The Gossler Guide to the
Best Hardy Shrubs

The Gossler Guide to the Best Hardy Shrubs

*More than 350
Expert Choices for
Your Garden*

Roger, Eric, and Marjory Gossler

Foreword by *John E. Elsley*

Timber Press
Portland | London

Page 1: *Hamamelis ×intermedia* 'Jelena'.

Frontispiece: In the "stream garden" part of our landscape, shrubs mingle with trees and perennials to create year-round interest.

Page 6: *Chaenomeles ×superba* 'Hollandia'.

Published in 2009 by Timber Press, Inc.

The Haseltine Building
133 S.W. Second Avenue, Suite 450
Portland, Oregon 97204-3527
www.timberpress.com

2 The Quadrant
135 Salusbury Road
London NW6 6RJ
www.timberpress.co.uk

Printed in China

Library of Congress Cataloging-in-Publication Data

Gossler, Roger.
    The Gossler guide to the best hardy shrubs : more than 350 expert choices for your garden / Roger, Eric, and Marjory Gossler ; foreword by John Elsley. — 1st ed.
        p. cm.
    Includes bibliographical references and index.
    ISBN 978-0-88192-908-9
    1. Ornamental shrubs. 2. Landscape gardening. I. Gossler, Eric. II. Gossler, Marjory. III. Title. IV. Title: Guide to the best hardy shrubs.
    SB435.G685 2009
    635.9'76—dc22
                                                                        2009006146

A catalog record for this book is also available from the British Library.

GOSSLER FARMS
NURSERY Est. 1968
Specializing In:

MAGNOLIAS DOGWOODS WITCHHAZELS
HYDRANGEAS AND OTHER COMPANION PLANTS

OPEN FOR DROP INS
FOR HOURS CONTACT US AT 746-3922

Visit
Us At: www.gosslerfarms.com

Contents

Foreword

THE HORTICULTURAL and gardening industry has witnessed dramatic changes in recent decades, especially in the marketing of plants. Large numbers of a limited range of plants are now sold through national and regional chain stores, causing smaller retail outlets to be challenged when they attempt to offer a broader selection of more unusual garden-worthy subjects. For many years, mail-order companies have been able to satisfy many of the needs of more serious gardeners, but recent economic fluctuations, combined with a possible decrease in demand for more esoteric offerings, has caused pressure on these sources as well.

Considering this sobering industry backdrop, Gossler Farms Nursery, a small, highly respected, forty-year-old, family-owned and -operated business is to be congratulated for their remarkable achievement. Their success can be attributed to the Gossler family's dedication to the nursery and its clientele—a factor frequently emphasized in the nursery catalog's introduction where the reader is addressed in a friendly and inclusive manner. Family activities and travels are discussed along with new plant introductions and pertinent nursery "chatter," leaving customers with a warm feeling of personal involvement. This feeling is further experienced when a telephone call to the nursery is inevitably answered by one of the owners. A conscientious commitment not to outgrow their resources ensures the ongoing production of quality plants and customer satisfaction. The hallmark of any Gossler Farms Nursery shipment is the uniquely successful method of firmly securing each plant in a "cat's cradle" before placing it in its shipping carton.

Roger Gossler's domestic and overseas travels ensure a steady supply of new and exciting offerings. Magnolias have always been a major specialty, with Japanese maples, rhododendrons, hydrangeas, and witch hazels representing other key groups. I am frequently recommending their catalog as a source for such hard-to-locate subjects as *Aralia elata* 'Variegata', unusual daphnes, and other unusual choices. Brevity and honesty typify catalog descriptions. In describing the exotic Chilean fire bush (*Embothrium coccineum*), it refreshingly states, "If you live out of the coastal Northwest from San Francisco to Vancouver, B.C., don't attempt this plant!"

Opposite: *Magnolia liliiflora* 'O'Neill'.

I first discovered Gossler Farms Nursery in my capacity as product development manager for Wayside Gardens. Subsequent visits have only enhanced my initial positive impressions and have led to a treasured friendship with Marj, Roger, and Eric. Regardless of season and weather, each visit is an exciting learning experience. Magnolias are the highlight of a spring tour of the beautiful and comprehensive display gardens, provided an unwelcome frost does not spoil the party. Weather can certainly be detrimental to garden visits to Oregon, yet one of my most memorable experiences of their gardens occurred on a dull, wet October day when the overcast conditions spectacularly enhanced a stunning fall color display. I especially recall the spectacular purple-leaved grape (*Vitis vinifera* 'Purpurea'), informally scrambling through the choice Japanese maple *Acer japonica* 'Aconitifolium' in full fall glory! My own South Carolina garden is enriched by several Gossler treasures which are a constant reminder of their Oregon origins. Foremost among them is a mature specimen of *Magnolia campbellii* 'Lanarth', a truly spectacular tree in full bloom. I am told by a leading authority that it is probably the only specimen of its kind on the entire East Coast. It took an excess of 15 years to produce its first bloom. *Camellia* ×*williamsii* 'Donation' is a prolific annual bloomer yet surprisingly uncommon in American gardens. I would not like to be without the graceful peacock camellia (*Camellia japonica* 'Kujaku-tsubaki'), whose weeping branches display red and white shuttlecock-like blossoms over an extended period in the spring.

Exploring the pages of this informative volume, we become acquainted with many of the plants that have inspired the Gosslers. By making these plants available, they create joy and beauty in the lives of countless gardeners—may the Gosslers continue their mission for many years to come.

JOHN E. ELSLEY
Greenwood, South Carolina

Acknowledgments

OVER THE COURSE of our operation we have been lucky enough to meet and befriend hundreds of gardeners from around the country. Some nurseries would consider this relationship to be simply that of business and customer, but in our case, many of those who visit our nursery have become long-term friends. We have visited some of their gardens while on vacation, and they in turn have visited us here at the nursery. We would like all of them to know how important these encounters have been over the years, and how much we always look forward to seeing and hearing from them.

The three of us have also been blessed with belonging to some wonderful local and national plant organizations. Without mentioning them individually, we would like to thank all the brave souls out there willing to take the time to run these public organizations and to tolerate the politics that often go along with such an operation. Through these organizations, we have become acquainted with hundreds of individuals without whom our lives would be much less interesting.

Finally, Eric's wife, Dawn, deserves a special thank you for her willingness to carry on living with a nursery owner. Operating a nursery is an alternative lifestyle in many ways—you rarely receive a regular paycheck, and your schedule can be frenzied, depending on plant sales, deliveries, and weather. For Dawn's willingness to support this lifestyle choice, and for her never-ending understanding, Eric remains eternally grateful.

Introduction

THIS PROJECT IS our effort to better your understanding of the use of shrubs in the landscape. Along the way, we hope to enable you to avoid some of the mistakes we have made and take advantage of our more than forty years of experience in the gardening and nursery trade. We also aim to provide some entertaining moments, coupled with helpful secrets to make your own experiences in the garden more enjoyable. We are currently at a crossroads in gardening and need to make absolutely sure we don't allow ourselves to become complacent. The availability of unique plant material is at an all-time high—we need to take advantage of this and encourage one another as gardeners to constantly push the envelope. We also need to help bring gardening to our neighbors and the communities around us. How do we do this? Plant new and unusual specimens for all to see. Sometimes all it takes is one house on a street doing something different, and the rest will follow suit. Try to grow specimen plants that spark interest and lead to discussions about the plants' identity and origin.

In 2007 we attended a plant sale in Seattle, at which a friend displayed *Calycanthus* ×*raulstonii* 'Hartlage Wine' in full bloom in her booth. Perhaps twenty people asked her where she had found the plant and how they could get one for themselves. Even though she did not carry it herself, she was able to steer these people in the right direction. This just goes to show what a single plant can do in your landscape if it is capable of distinguishing itself from the crowd. We see this time and again in our own garden: people are intrigued by unusual plants, which almost always sparks a discussion.

If you were to drive through any of the newer housing developments around the United States, you would see the same twenty plant species grown, all of which may have come from the same twenty growers. This is a sad fact when there is so much material out there with which gardeners can distinguish themselves. It also creates a monoculture of sorts, which can lead to diversity problems when it comes to diseases and climate variations. Right now around the country hundreds of thousands of red maples are planted every month as street trees. Think about it the next time you drive through a maple-lined neighborhood: most of

Opposite: Plants with dazzling fall foliage, such as *Acer palmatum* var. *dissectum* 'Crimson Queen' (foreground) and *Stewartia koreana* (background), often spark discussion.

these trees come from the same genetic pool. If a problem ever arises, all of these maples could be lost at once. We have seen this before with Dutch elm disease and other problems.

Many municipalities around the United States have exceedingly limited lists of approved varieties for street and public plantings. These lists are often outdated and lacking in diversity. In our area, we know of customers who have placed a false tag on a plant, deliberately misidentifying it to avoid complying with the approved city list. Plants should not be forced into a witness protection program in order to survive. Nor should people be forced to cheat and lie just to plant something different.

Another sad fact is that while the size of the average house is growing, the average lot size is shrinking, thereby forcing many new homeowners to adopt a cookie-cutter planting scheme because of lack of space. This especially affects the use of larger specimen trees, since many lots just don't have room for them. Customers frequently ask us whether a tree that ultimately grows to 30 feet (9 m) tall can be planted 4 feet (1.2 m) from a house. When we tell them no, the follow-

Callicarpa bodinieri var. *giraldii* 'Profusion' is another attention-getter, grown for its colorful fruit.

up question is almost always the same: "Can we prune it?" We understand their frustration, although we ourselves are lucky enough to have the space needed to display large specimens. While helping some friends with their landscaping recently, we struggled with the square shape of their city lot. It was difficult to come up with options that did not look like the little strip plantings that all the neighbors have. In the end, however, we had the other people on the street asking about the unusual plants in our friends' garden. What we all need to understand is that there are thousands of smaller shrubs available, each one willing to give us its all if it is only given the chance to perform.

We are constantly evaluating new plant material and are amazed by the amount of new varieties available each year. You would think that at some point all available combinations for a certain species would be exhausted, yet each season spectacular offerings continue to come to the public. One example is *Davidia involucrata* 'Sonoma'. This plant is so superior to its predecessors that it is almost like a separate species. The flowers are roughly three times larger than those of past varieties, and the blooming age was taken from perhaps fifteen years to two. Considering this example, you can never become too comfortable with what you think you know about any given genus.

The amount of shrubs available today is astounding compared to the late 1990s. The Internet has provided most everyone with direct access to the specialty nurseries that carry these new and exciting varieties. As for us, we are spoiled with our large display garden of roughly 4 acres, which is stuffed full. Even so, we are constantly faced with deciding what plants must be cut down and removed to make room for new varieties. This kind of decision is even more difficult for the average gardener limited by a smaller space. We hope to help with this by exposing you to these plants and helping you digest what will work best in your own garden. We too have planted the coveted new treasure in the garden, giving it a place of honor and pampering it for years only to have it bloom the wrong color or die after the first cold winter. This happens to the best of us. Experimentation can be exciting, however, because for every plant that doesn't live up to your hopes and dreams, ten more exceed them.

The shrubs we discuss in this book are those we feel represent the best of each genus. We have selected plants that have the greatest possible chance of success in a variety of climates and locations around the country. We have personally grown almost every plant we describe and feel comfortable recommending them. Our garden is more than forty years old. It contains around six thousand plant varieties, and the list is always changing as we evaluate new plants for the market. In some cases we decide a plant is not worth continuing to grow due to its difficulty of cultivation. In other cases a plant proves itself to be invasive or a pest in some other way. Our aim is to help you learn from our experiences and feel comfortable selecting interesting new shrubs for your own space.

So many cultivars come to the market at such a fast pace that it is difficult to sort through them, even if you have a large garden and are in the nursery trade as we are. At times, however, new selections can be inferior to the older standards, in which case we say that newer isn't necessarily better. Sometimes, in an effort to be novel, a nursery fails to ask whether a plant is worthy before putting it into production. For example, many of the newer *Hamamelis* varieties are inferior to the older standards in terms of color, fragrance, and flower size. If you are a col-

Gardeners have an astonishing number of choices when it comes to ornamental hardy shrubs. In this late-spring scene from our garden, *Chionanthus virginicus* and other shrubs provide a lush background for perennials.

lector and have room for twenty different specimens that are 12 feet (3.6 m) across, you might want to acquire some of the new cultivars; but most gardeners only have room for one or two plants, and in this case we generally steer them to one of the older varieties.

Smaller specialty nurseries can be found almost everywhere these days; they offer some wonderful options and can be a treasure trove of information if you are willing to explore off the beaten track. In contrast, many of the plants available at the big-box stores and largest garden centers will not be suited for your climate, and the salespeople often lack the experience to answer even basic questions. The Internet, for those willing to surf, is an invaluable tool, making information available that used to take years to compile or be impossible to find altogether.

Our nursery is our livelihood, but it started as a hobby born out of our love for plants. Our goal in this book is to expose you, our fellow gardeners, to the latest, most exciting plant varieties and help you develop your own unique gardening style. We also hope to be a little entertaining along the way. So sit back, put your feet up, pour a glass of your beverage of choice, and enjoy.

How to Think about Climate and Growing Conditions

THE WILLAMETTE VALLEY of Oregon, where our nursery is located, is perhaps one of the best places in the country to raise and test plants from around the globe. In our climate, we are able to mimic the conditions of Asia and other parts of the world to at least some degree.

The Willamette Valley is tempered by the Pacific Ocean, and therefore the climate is relatively moderate. We receive 40–50 inches of rain per year on average, but the bulk of that falls between November and April. It is not uncommon to go two or three months with zero precipitation during the summer. This surprises many of our visitors, who stubbornly cling to the idea that western Oregon is one large rain forest. In fact we rarely surpass 30 percent humidity in the summer, and on most nights the temperature drops into the fifties even when we are seeing daytime highs in the mid nineties. It is this nightly cooling and lower humidity that set us apart from the rest of the country.

As with any other part of the world, we have had our share of weather nightmares. In the winter of 1972 we reached an all-time low of –12°F (–24°C). This was devastating to say the least, considering that our usual winter low is in the high teens. At the time of the freeze we were heavily involved in species rhododendrons, and an enormous portion of them died within a few days. This turned out to be a blessing in disguise, however, because it allowed us to go in a different direction and increase our planting diversity. We came to believe that you should never rely heavily on any one genus as the backbone of your landscape. Accordingly, over the following years and decades we experimented with a vast array of plants from around the world. Many of these varieties now comprise the bulk of our garden. Of course, this is not to say that another extreme freeze would not be devastating, but the majority of our plants would certainly have a greater chance for survival.

Our personal tormentor is the McKenzie River, which we live beside. On February 8, 1996, our entire nursery was under water, as was about 70 percent of our display garden. This was not stagnant water but white water. An aerial photo of our land appeared on the national news as a symbol of the devastation. (If you

---

Opposite: Every garden has its own microclimate. In this sunny spot, spiky phormiums provide a focal point in front of shrubs that will strut their color later in the season.

A diverse landscape is a healthy landscape. In this area of our garden, hostas, shrubs, and trees commingle at the edge of a lawn.

ever want a bad night's sleep, try imagining your entire livelihood floating away toward the Pacific.)

We share these stories to show you that the Northwest, like most places, has its weather demons; and like everyone else, we have been forced to be adaptable when it comes to dealing with Mother Nature. We are sure to face many more challenges in the future, as the threat of climate change looms large. If changes in the weather take place over generations, plants may have time to adapt, but if they happen quickly, we will be forced to get more creative when it comes to designing and planting our gardens.

We always encourage our customers to experiment with plants that are on the edge of their hardiness zone. Just don't make the mistake we made so many years ago by relying on one genus or zone capability to dominate your garden.

We see remarkable variation in what people can grow within just a few miles of one another, so experiment to see what works best for you in your particu-

Camellia ×williamsii 'Donation' is perhaps the best camellia for the climate of the Pacific Northwest.

lar microclimate. We have a very large magnolia collection, and each year the blooming can be affected by frost. Within half a mile of our garden at the same elevation is a public park planted with a large assortment of magnolias. Although these trees are within sight of our garden, year after year they suffer from frost damage while our specimens of the same varieties remain unharmed. This is simply due to a cold pocket in the park. Should the park planners cut all of these trees down and start over? They simply need to adapt their plantings and look for later-blooming, more frost-resistant magnolia varieties. The problem as we see it is that people often fail to notice the evidence when it comes to learning about the climatic conditions of their own site.

When visitors to our garden ask about our "master" plan or design, we jokingly reply, "Darwinism." We have a large space and maintain it with little staff help. We do this by allowing the plants to make some of the decisions for themselves. It doesn't make sense to force a plant into the wrong situation, since it ends up being more work for both the gardener and the plant. We estimate that there are between five and six thousand plant varieties in our garden. If we were providing for the individual care of each plant, we would never be able to just sit back and enjoy the process. Therefore, when we find that a plant can't thrive in a given location or is struggling in any way, we remove it and either try planting it in another location or else simply move on. It is not worth the time and effort to fight against nature. From time to time we decide that a plant we are offering for sale is too difficult to grow and raise in a normal garden setting, in which case we remove it from our stock, because we feel it is not worth the struggle.

The big advantage we have here is that we have lived in the same location for more than fifty years and are naturalized to it. What are you to do, though, if you move to a new state, or even just the other side of town? There will always be an adjustment period when you find yourself outside your comfort zone. One of the first things you should do, if possible, is research the climate of the new area. This simple process can save enormous time and stress when it comes to selecting plants. Local groups and gardening organizations are great tools, capable of providing endless amounts of information and allowing you to learn from others' mistakes and triumphs. The final all-important task is to start early with building your own personal history for your property. Each little piece of this planet has its own attributes that need to be accounted for. The more you add to your own history, the more you can branch out and grow along with your plants.

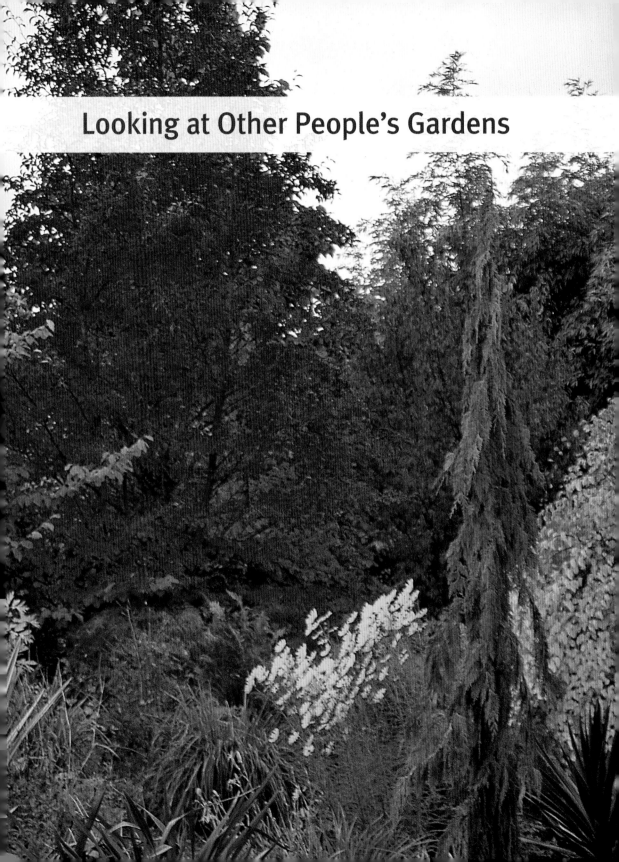

Looking at Other People's Gardens

OVER THE COURSE of forty-plus years of collecting plants and operating a nursery, our style and selections have been affected by a myriad of influences. Each time we encounter another garden it changes our perspective and causes us to look differently at our own situation. We have been fortunate to have worked with and befriended some of the gardening pioneers of the Pacific Northwest and other parts of the country. Some of these people have had a profound influence on our ideas about gardening and have helped us become what we are today. Of course, there have also been times when we have looked at other gardens and seen what we didn't want to become. We will discuss this aspect of influence as well, with the hope that you will be able to use what we have learned to help shape your own situation.

One of our earliest and most significant influences was the late Jane Platt. We met Jane when she came to the nursery in 1968. Our nursery was firmly on the hobby side of the fence; we had a small number of selections, and everything was housed under one wooden lathhouse. At the time we thought we had quite the selection of plants, having no idea what was truly available. Most of our inventory was comprised of magnolias and rhododendrons, and we grew roughly half an acre of street trees for the local market. Jane and her husband, John, arrived the morning of February 24, purchased a large number of plants, and asked if it would be possible to have them delivered to the Portland area. Agreeing to deliver that first load of plants proved to be one of our best decisions in our decades of gardening. From this visit we formed an alliance with Jane that lasted for many years. It was a relationship that exposed us to vast arrays of new plants and garden designs, opening our eyes to endless options and opportunities.

The Platts lived in the West Hills of Portland. Their house had been designed by Pietro Belluschi and was stunning in the way it melded into its hillside location. It seemed to grow out of the garden, with stone walls and natural barn wood siding. The interior was comprised of expansive natural slate floors and large windows overlooking the landscape. At the time we had never visited a gar-

---

Opposite: This mixed shrub border boasts a diversity of plant structures, fall colors, and foliage types, combining large plants like *Stewartia koreana* and *Chamaecyparis nootkatensis* with various shrubs and perennials.

den of that size, maturity, and class. We were stunned by the variety of plants and were eager for a tour.

After admiring the individual plants, we marveled at the grace and beauty of the overall landscape. It showed us what could be done and gave us fantastic ideas about how to accomplish it. Prior to this time we had mainly visited gardens made up of collections of single genera—one would focus on rhododendrons, another on magnolias, and so on. This was our first real view of a truly blended garden in which plants worked together to create a complete scene. It was our personal awakening as gardeners, and from that point on we tried to incorporate various aspects of what we had seen during these visits into our own landscape.

Thanks to the influence of gardeners like Jane Platt, we have learned to combine multiple elements to create a unified garden. In this scene, the greenish yellow leaves of *Acer shirasawanum* 'Aureum' glow atop a bed of hostas and other perennials.

We will always be grateful for the time we spent with Jane, the influence she had on our garden, and the effect she had in shaping what direction we took in the selection of plants for our nursery. She undoubtedly had no idea how much of an impact she had. Though she is no longer with us, if she were somehow able to visit our garden tomorrow, we would hope she would appreciate the feel of it, because she helped to shape it.

Another influence on our selections and designs was Western Hills Nursery in Occidental, California, which has been a mecca for unusual plants since the early 1970s. In the late 1950s, Lester Hawkins and Marshall Olbrich moved to Occidental, a tiny town west of Sebastopol. A two-hour drive from San Francisco, Occidental might as well have been a thousand miles away, for the difference at the time was profound. Hawkins and Olbrich moved there intending to build a homestead, growing their own food and becoming self-sufficient. They built a simple wood and adobe house and added a number of small outbuildings. When growing all their own food didn't pan out, they started raising and selling seed plants from all parts of the world, ranging from Australian and African plants to hundreds of California natives. This was the start of their experimentation. To this day they have some of the largest specimens in the United States of certain unusual plants, including *Acer pentaphyllum* and *Cornus controversa* 'Variegata'.

The Western Hills garden is located in a small canyon just over the hill from the Pacific Ocean, a canyon so tight that the garden is compressed by the hillside from seemingly all directions. One of its more unique aspects is that it includes no lawn grass. Instead it is a maze of small winding paths weaving through the canyon. The paths have been improved with bridges over a small seasonal creek that flows through the landscape. The creek has been contained in a series of rock-lined channels to cut down on erosion taking place during heavy rains.

Roger first visited Western Hills in 1974. He was stunned by the diversity of plants and intrigued by the way they were used in this unique setting with narrow paths and no lawns. At that time a garden generally included a large lawn with a few plants around the edges. Western Hills was far from the traditional model to which Roger had become accustomed. He became excited about incorporating some of these new ideas into our own landscape. He was also stunned with the use of plants from the Southern Hemisphere, something few people were trying at the time. It was enlightening to see these strange and unusual plants mixed together with traditional plants from Asia and Europe.

We would be remiss if we did not discuss another influence: the late J. C. Raulston, director of the North Carolina State University Arboretum (now the J. C. Raulston Arboretum) in the 1980s and 1990s. Anyone who knew J. C.

would remember the feverish pace at which he lived his life. Over a relatively short period of time, he helped bring hundreds of new plants into the nursery trade. J. C. would tell us, "This plant is wonderful. You need to be selling it!" He did the same with other nurseries around the country, becoming the Johnny Appleseed of new and unusual plants. He felt that new material was not something to keep to yourself but rather something to be shared as quickly as possible with the gardening public. J. C. approached the promotion of plants from a holistic standpoint, encouraging those who attended his lectures to ask their local retailers to sell a certain plant. He would even go to the retailer himself and say, "Look, people are asking for this plant." This pied piper approach helped improve the accessibility of many of the plants we carry today.

Our "stream garden," seen here in summer, incorporates some of the ideas we first encountered years ago at Western Hills and other innovative gardens. Bamboo in a Thai pottery container adds another unique element.

J. C. also turned the North Carolina State University Arboretum into one of the premier arboretums of the United States. He traveled the world to find new plants, then brought them back for trials to determine whether they were worthy of release to the public. During that time we regularly received packages of plants to grow, propagate, and sell to our customers. There is no way to tell how many varieties would remain unavailable today if it had not been for the efforts J. C. made in distributing material. One of the plants we received has a sad but great story. When the natural tetraploid *Styrax japonicus* 'Emerald Pagoda' was discovered growing wild in Korea, a few scions were collected. The group who found the plant returned two years later to obtain more seeds, but the area had been logged and the source tree was gone. From these first few scions, only a limited number of plants survived. J. C. gave us one of these plants under the condition we would try to propagate it for the trade. That was in the mid 1980s, and now 'Emerald Pagoda' is widely grown around the country.

Unfortunately J. C. was killed in a car crash in 1997, ending his meteoric run in the plant community. If he was still with us, there would be many more new and exciting plants out there for all of us to enjoy.

We have encountered many other influential figures during our evolution as gardeners and horticulturists. We encourage you, too, to visit other gardens even if it is something you would never normally consider doing. All the information you gather will help expand and shape your individual style.

What is perhaps the hardest thing for us to see here at the nursery are the customers who come in with "the list." They have hired a designer and have resigned themselves to having no personal effect on their own garden. They make their way through the nursery with all the joy of someone checking off a grocery list (eggs, aisle four; bread, aisle two; dish soap, aisle ten; and so on). Having a professional help with the general layout is sometimes useful, especially if you have never tackled starting from scratch or if you have a large landscape. But when it comes to choosing plants, it is *your* taste and emotions that need to be satisfied, not the designer's. After all, you are the one who has to live with the final product. We can't tell you how many times we have heard customers say, "That is spectacular, but unfortunately it is not on the list." Shopping for plants this way is like dating on the Internet: it may sound good, but until you are face to face you don't know if you have really found the one! The same is true with plant selection. Just because the designer likes it doesn't necessarily mean that you will.

The various plant groups around the country are another great resource. These groups abound and are a wealth of information and ideas. Our local group brings together people from all walks of life, with many different styles and

Opposite: Every garden, like every gardener, has its own personality. In this section of our woodland garden, sculptures by local artist Ray Beard echo the large leaves of a gunnera.

ideas, to discuss plants and design. Such groups also frequently offer tours of gardens in the area, which can be invaluable when it comes to seeing what is out there and deciding what will work for you personally. Many plant groups also invite guest lecturers from around the world who share even more new and exciting information.

The main idea we want to stress is the importance of forming your own opinion on design and personalizing your landscape to your taste—even if you are the only one who can tolerate it, at least it reflects your own dreams. Also, if you are starting a garden from scratch, don't feel that it has to be done all at once. Take your time and experiment with locations and layouts. This is where some of your best ideas may originate. Don't expect your garden to be the way you are going to have it for the next twenty years on the first attempt; it may take several tries to find what works. We are constantly changing our landscape and working on ways to improve it. This sometimes means sacrificing mature specimens to make a change. Every once in a while we get it right, and it is worth the effort and sacrifice.

Our Personal Guide to Plant Categories

WHEN DECIDING what plants to include in this book, we applied the same criteria we use when selecting plants for our garden. These criteria can be broken down into the following categories:

Old war horses
Standards
New kids on the block
Just plain fun
Tender mercies
Oddities

While these labels might be somewhat tongue in cheek, there are valid reasons for including each category in the landscape. Used together, these plant groups paint an overall mosaic. We have spent the better part of our time since the late 1960s discovering what works in our garden and deciding which plants our customers might like to purchase. This can be a tough tightrope to walk, but it can also be exciting when it all comes together. As you consider these categories, the two most important things to remember are that our "rules" may be different from yours, and all rules are meant to be broken at some point.

Old war horses

These are the plants we all know and love, plants frequently seen in older, established gardens. They should never be forgotten, particularly since they are so often the parents and grandparents of newer, somewhat flashier members of the landscape. One example is *Pieris japonica*. This species has been around since the earth cooled, and yet it still works. It is also a parent of many of the more modern and showy *Pieris* available today. *Pieris japonica* is what we consider a classic beauty. Don't fall for the idea that newer is always better: know and study these older standards and use them to your advantage.

Opposite: *Chionanthus virginicus* in summer.

Standards

These are the plants grown on a massive scale by some of the largest growers in the country. They are the plants you find everywhere, at garden centers, nurseries, and sometimes even supermarkets.

The largest agricultural business in Oregon is the nursery trade. Some of the biggest nurseries in the entire country are located here. While driving by one such nursery recently, we noticed a sign saying "main gate one mile ahead"; this was fine, but we had already been driving past their operation for over a mile. These large nurseries raise hundreds of thousands of a single cultivar without blinking an eye. This is not to say that this is wrong in any way. Large nurseries are simply raising the standards, plants that have remained marketable around the country for years or even decades.

Viburnum ×bodnantense 'Dawn', for example, is mass-produced nationally and yet remains an outstanding performer in any garden. We normally shy away from growing material raised by these large growers because it is difficult to keep up with the mass-production style and assembly-line process in which they operate. This *Viburnum*, however, is one that we will always carry.

New kids on the block

Every season there is a new rock star that everyone must have. These plants are grown for their fifteen minutes of fame, although they sometimes disappear from the scene just as fast. They are often spectacular. Gardeners put their names on waiting lists to own one and want all their friends to know when the plant finally arrives. There can be a downside, however: we have actually had customers receive a long-awaited plant only to come out the next morning and find it stolen right out of the ground!

One such plant is the stunning *Calycanthus ×raulstonii* 'Hartlage Wine', a cross between *C. floridus* and *C. chinensis* developed at North Carolina State University. Of course, celebrity status is fleeting; by the time you read this, twenty more rock stars will have seen their moment in the sun.

Calycanthus ×raulstonii 'Hartlage Wine'.

Just plain fun

Plants in this group are not the showiest or the most well known; they are the plants you grow just because they are entertaining. Some of these should always be worked in just for the discussion they generate when visitors tour the garden. We have just such a plant near our office, *Ilex crenata* 'Dwarf Pagoda'. It is always entertaining to ask people what they think this simple plant might be. Occasionally someone identifies it correctly, but most people are amazed to learn that it is a holly. Our plant is roughly forty years old and only 4 feet (1.2 m) high. Its compressed habit makes the branches almost seem as if they are made of spring-tempered steel. There are no thorns, and the leaves are only ¼ inch (0.6 cm) across. These details leave most visitors stumped. Now, is this the showiest plant? No. But is it worth having, just to be different? Yes. If you find this type of plant during your travels, try to find room for it in your garden. It will be worth it for the entertainment and conversation that it generates.

Ilex crenata 'Dwarf Pagoda', right, with *Picea abies* 'Pendula'.

Tender mercies

Now to the sometimes touchy subject of pushing the zonal envelope, a category we call tender mercies. On the day you put these plants in the ground, you know the clock has started and it is only a matter of time before Mother Nature comes calling. The question is whether there will be enough of an emotional reward to get you through the grief that invariably comes with incorporating such plants in the garden. Some of the plants we grow are certain to be lost in a hard winter, but we stick with them because the rewards are so great.

Embothrium coccineum is a prime example. We have raised this Chilean plant in our garden for decades and realize that we will lose it every few years. It makes a spectacular show when in bloom, its brilliant crimson flowers visible from hundreds of yards away against the dark black-green leaves. Now to the reality of

Late spring in our garden, with *Embothrium coccineum*, center, ablaze amidst rhododendrons and other shrubs.

the equation: we can expect our *E. coccineum* to die whenever temperatures drop below 0°F (–18°C). Every time we lose a plant, we plant a new one, just hoping it will get large enough to bloom before its number is up.

The trick with tender mercies is to never let them become the foundation of your landscape. Like chocolate and other decadent sweets, they should be enjoyed in moderation.

Oddities

Now for the oddities, specimens you grow just because they are so different from everything else. These plants simply inspire astonishment. Every garden needs at least one as a conversation piece.

Several years ago we visited the Philadelphia area and, like good sheep, dropped in on all the standard tourist attractions. However, we had also heard that the College of Physicians of Philadelphia housed something called the Mütter Museum, a little-known attraction just blocks from Independence Hall and other heavily traveled sites. To find this museum, we had to know what we were looking for—it is located in the basement of the college's administration building. Once inside, we had the feeling we had stepped into a sideshow from an old traveling carnival. Each of us went from display case to display case trying to decide whether we were more repulsed or intrigued by what we were viewing, saying to each other, "Get over here and look at this!"

Now, while this particular experience might not be for everyone, there is sometimes a need for this same effect in the garden. We sometimes use plants not because they are beautiful but because we want to draw people into the garden. One such oddity is *Poncirus trifoliata* 'Flying Dragon'—never the belle of the ball, but definitely an attention-getter. With its large, fish-hooked, curling thorns and lack of any normal foliage, 'Flying Dragon' is a wicked-looking package. As long as an oddity like this is used judiciously, it can work to your advantage.

We list only one example in each plant category because ultimately your own taste and climate will be the deciding factors. We strongly believe there should never be solid rules in gardening—as with any other art form, it should come down to personal choice. In the end, if your garden gets you and your visitors thinking and enjoying the overall experience, that is all that matters.

The categories listed here are simple, but each can be applied to the more than six thousand varieties of plants that reside in our own garden. If you were to walk our grounds, you could probably check off the appropriate box for each plant and know where it fits in our scheme. The key is to never rely on any single category as the framework of your landscape. (Sorry, we know we said earlier that there should be no rules.)

We have visited many gardens over the years, and reliance on just one category is all too common. Gardeners will pigeonhole themselves into a category, counting much too heavily on a single aspect and thus limiting the overall vision. They sometimes also set themselves up for disaster by relying on Mother Nature to behave herself. When the devastating winter of 1972 wiped out our rhododendron collection, rhododendrons were the basis of our entire landscape, and we were forced to rebuild a good portion of the garden. Trust us when we say that you never want to go through this experience.

Another issue not often covered is budget. Many gardening books discuss plants as if you were operating with a 25-million-dollar endowment for a 75-by-100-foot city lot. We understand that most people cannot operate on an unlimited budget. By blending the plant categories we have described, you can accomplish some wonderful things without sacrificing your ability to buy food at the end of each month. Many of the plants in the first two categories (old war horses, standards) are available almost anywhere at a reasonable price. We have found, after years of growing nursery stock, that bigger is not always better. A plant in a large container or one that is field grown and root balled will often sit in the ground for several seasons just trying to catch its breath. Meanwhile a somewhat smaller containerized plant will often take off immediately, catching up with the bigger plant and ultimately surpassing it. If you are starting a garden from scratch, it may be advantageous to scatter around a few bigger items in the beginning. On the whole, however, starting with a smaller plant provides the desired look almost as fast and for much less money.

How Not to Kill Your Plants

THE JOB OF KEEPING your carefully acquired treasures alive once you receive a shipment or return from your local nursery is often where things go terribly wrong. In the world of medicine, the term "golden hour" refers to the time immediately following an accident or injury, when the patient's survivability is greatly affected by whatever intervention takes place. Plants can be thought of in the same way: if time is mismanaged at the beginning, the ultimate success of the plant will be in jeopardy.

It starts with the selection of the individual plant, which can be tricky. The best advice here is to choose a supplier you know and trust when it comes to how they raise their plants. This applies to mail-order operations as well: pay attention to reputation, and talk to your friends to see how plants are packaged and handled.

Several years ago we had a problem after receiving an order of *Choisya ternata* 'Sundance'. At first glance the plants looked fabulous, but when we took one of them out of its pot to place in the garden, we found that it had almost no roots whatsoever. There was nothing more than a large callus with several hair-sized roots coming out of it. On further inspection the entire block proved to be in the same condition. This was the result of a fairly common practice: the nursery in question watered its plants with a mist system in a heated greenhouse, forcing liquid fertilizer through the system on each watering cycle. The plants had never had to grow actual roots to support their growth rate because everything was handed to them. Before we could sell our plants to the public, we had to cut them back to about half their original size, which allowed them to grow roots and balance themselves out from top to bottom.

What often happens is that you see an incredibly lush plant in a garden center and, thinking how healthy it looks, automatically expect it to perform as well in your own garden, only to find that it struggles there. This is akin to taking an animal that was raised in captivity and releasing it into the wild with the expectation that it will hunt and forage on its own. The animal will eventually wither and starve without help, and the same is true of these garden center plants. In an effort to maximize production, large wholesale growers often force plants at a rate

Opposite: *Cornus sanguinea* 'Midwinter Fire'.

so far outside their natural growth pattern that the consumer can never hope to keep up this pace. So what can you do? First, note whether the plant looks like a competitive bodybuilder or an East German female shot putter from the 1970s. If so, know that you may need to help it learn to survive on its own. We often aggressively prune the tops of newly arrived plants before planting or potting them, which helps balance the root structure with the foliage. The same plants may also need additional watering and fertilizer during the first season until they can adapt to life on their own. Don't be afraid to trim heavily in the beginning; it is better to have a new plant loaded underground with roots, and the plant will have a chance to catch up on top the next season. Aggressive pruning can also stimulate the plant into a growth spurt once it is comfortable with its new surroundings.

Plants should not look like they have been in the same container for the last ten years with little or no new growth. Many plants will only grow to the size of their surroundings—in this case, the container. If left in a container too long, they will almost stop all new growth, and once this occurs it is difficult to get growth to restart. Once again, pruning can be the answer, as this can potentially stimulate new growth. It is also important to loosen the roots, allowing them to break free of their bondage and roam free in the soil.

In a society in which the goal is to be as "green" as possible, it frustrates us that so many gardeners seem to want their plants to look like Miss America contestants. The largest nurseries push fertilizer, herbicides, and insecticides at a rate that would horrify the average retail customer if they only knew. Earlier we mentioned a nursery that went on for miles; along that same road, we also noticed a ditch leading away from the nursery that was absolutely devoid of life—it might as well have been the surface of the moon. The question is whether you should go entirely organic. The answer is ultimately up to the individual gardener, but we suggest that you ask yourself what you would do if you owned a nursery, and then look for those same characteristics in the growers you support. At our nursery, we try to find a balance between the needs of the plants and the realities of running a commercial operation. We try as hard as we can to use chemicals only when absolutely necessary and only in targeted applications, and we use fertilizer only in the amount we feel will promote normal growth rates in the plants we raise.

Several years ago we had an insect problem in one of the plant varieties we carried. We tried spraying the plants several times with different chemicals, but the problem continued to pop up. When we began to ask around, we found that every grower was having similar problems with this particular variety. The only solution was to continue spraying the plants once a month without end. Upon learning this, we ordered a commercial dumpster and threw away every plant, sending them directly to the county landfill, pot soil and all. Other growers thought we were crazy, believing we could have managed the pest with insecticides. We disagreed. We didn't want to expose ourselves or our customers to that type of spraying regimen. Our solution was severe, but it worked and we never regretted it. Many larger nurseries apply pesticides each month whether or not there is any problem. Not only does this practice breed resistant strains of insects, it also completely removes the positive insects from the equation.

Another mistake gardeners regularly make is trying to raise containerized stock at home. Container stock needs large amounts of water during the growing season. These plants also tend to be moisture sensitive to the extreme, a need that most homeowners cannot meet. The potting mixes used in many nurseries do not hold water well and dry out rapidly. Most are comprised of almost all bark and sand. During the peak of summer we water our outside material at least once a day, and in extreme cases of heat and low humidity, this may be pushing it. Sometimes a person who is waiting to move into a new house decides to start buying nursery stock ahead of time and storing it. If these plants don't die altogether, they generally suffer, and then struggle once they reach their permanent home. We suggest holding off on buying plants until you are ready to place them directly in the ground with a functioning watering system.

Finally, don't be afraid to ask a grower how they raised the plants you are about to buy. Consider it an open adoption: you want to know about the birth parents, what neighborhood the plant came from, whether drugs were involved, and so on. These simple questions can affect the ultimate survival of any purchase. Always ask yourself when you are shopping, "Does this look like the plant I would grow if I had a small shade house and the right equipment?" If the answer is no, be prepared to help the plant transition from captivity to the wild.

Care and Maintenance

THIS ENDEAVOR would not be complete without discussing planting, pruning, mulching, and the timing of each of these events. We have a different take on some of these subjects and would like to share what has worked best for us. We have been grooming our display garden since the 1960s and in that time have developed many shortcuts and procedures that allow us to maintain it with minimal support staff. In this chapter we discuss these methods, but keep in mind that you may need to modify our schedule for your own environment and climate.

Where to plant your new treasure

Once you have a new plant in hand, you need to decide where to place it and how best to ensure its survival. Sometimes gardeners outthink themselves, worry-

---

Opposite: *Acer palmatum* 'Shishigashira' in fall.

Place shrubs where they are most likely to succeed. This *Hamamelis* thrives in partial shade with a host of perennials planted at its feet.

ing about too many variables rather than focusing simply on whether a plant will thrive in its chosen spot. Each plant variety has its own preferences. It is important to research these preferences and avoid forcing plants outside their zone of comfort.

We often place new plants, still in their containers, in the area we plan on planting them and leave them there for several days or even a week. This allows us to see whether the location will look right to us in the long run. If necessary, we keep moving the plants around like giant chess pieces until the design finally fits our eye.

Watering and drainage

Excessive moisture can be the single biggest killer of both new and mature plants. If possible, always plant in well-drained soil. Plants almost always struggle in a wet environment, and too much moisture will leave them susceptible to certain diseases and insect pests. The same thing can be true for established trees and shrubs. Over the years we have made various changes in our watering systems in different sections of the garden, such as starting to provide mature trees with regular water when in the past they only received water sporadically during summer. In several cases the change resulted in the loss of a mature plant. The tree had spent its entire life adapting its root structure to the drier environment in which it had resided, and when the water increased, it simply drowned.

A customer once came to us when his monkey puzzle tree (*Araucaria araucana*), the focal point in front of his house, was turning brown and dying. A local garden center had sent him home with sprays and insecticides, assuming the tree was under some kind of biological attack. When we looked at it ourselves, we could tell that the customer had recently remodeled the beds nearby and in the process had piled a mound of soil on top of the tree's roots. This was trapping water at the base of the tree and quickly killing it. The customer hadn't even considered this when remodeling the beds and was surprised to learn the true cause of the problem. Unfortunately, the tree was ultimately lost.

If you are forced to place a new plant in a wet environment, try to plant it in a mound above the surrounding soil. This way the plant can decide for itself how much water it needs and send its roots into the water supply as far as is appropriate. Many people place new plants too deep in the soil. If there is ever any question, it is better to plant a little too high than too low. If you have heavy clay soil, try to amend it before planting anything; the lighter soil will give the new plant room to grow its roots, and once it is stronger it will be able to push into the denser clay. Amending can be accomplished in several ways. Generally you need to break up the soil mechanically and then add sand mixed with some form of humus material that is either wood or peat based. This will need to be supplemented with a fertilizer that will combat either extreme alkalinity or extreme acidity while providing nourishment to the plant.

Many parts of the country are in the midst of some of the driest conditions of the last one hundred years, so it is no surprise that customers increasingly ask us about drought-tolerant plants. Many of the plants we discuss in this book need supplemental water to survive in most applications. However, if a plant is slowly transitioned, it will usually survive on a relatively small amount of extra water. We are blessed with the ability to supply our garden with however much water we desire, so this has never been a problem for us personally. Nevertheless, we continue to experiment with new drought-tolerant plants to meet the needs that many gardeners now face.

Site preparation

Over the years we have delivered plants to many locations and have seen everything from multimillion-dollar landscapes to the smallest, most modest gardens you can imagine. We have seen far too many gardeners make the mistake of failing to prepare their site prior to planting. After purchasing a new house or property, people are often so excited to start planting that they skip the necessary groundwork. They may intend to go back later on and clear out the native vegetation or amend the soil properly, but once they have planted sporadically in the area, it becomes difficult to perform these tasks without sacrificing the plants. If you are ever in this situation, take the time at the beginning to lay out a plan and do the necessary site preparation before the first plant hits the ground.

Preparation will be different in every situation. If you are starting with a new piece of ground, make sure that all your big hardscape features are in place: walkways, sculptures, sprinkler systems, and so forth. It will make your life much easier if you have these items in place before planting anything. On the other hand, if you are moving into an established garden there will already be a structure in place, in which case the important idea is to pick your battles. For starters, is the garden worth saving or do you need to start from scratch? If you are going to save it, break it into sections. Work on one area at a time so that you can focus your energy and finish each zone before moving on to the next. Sometimes, rather than focusing on one area, gardeners try to attack the entire landscape at once, and in the end never finish any single part of the project.

When building on their own site, people also sometimes allow their contractor to do the excavation without discussing the soil in the area. In many parts of the country there is only a thin layer of topsoil covering rock, clay, or other soils with little value for growing plants. Once this is scraped off or covered over, the gardener is placed in the undesirable situation of having to spend time and money to add what may have been there in the first place.

Several years ago a subdivision was built in the floodplain near our home. The builders were required to raise the area above the one-hundred-year floodplain before beginning construction. They excavated a barrow pit and used the excavated material to fill the area to a depth of several feet. In digging the pit, they went through 5–8 feet (1.5–2.4 m) of some of the most beautiful sandy loam you have ever seen. Once through this layer, they were into cobble rock that came from an old river channel, each rock about 3–6 inches (7.5–15 cm) in diameter. As you might guess, the good loam was placed down first, followed by the solid cobble rock. The owners of the new houses had to either haul in loam or make do with no topsoil, few of them ever aware of the beautiful soil beneath all that horrible rock.

Pruning techniques

Pruning can be frightening. Many gardeners seem to worry that if they make the wrong choice, the plant police will swoop down and issue a citation. For this reason, plants are sometimes allowed to take over like a bunch of unruly kindergarteners. This is unfortunate, because every plant in the garden should be evaluated each season to determine whether there is a need for thinning or shaping. We do all of our work in the winter and try to hit the period of maximum dormancy. This places the least amount of stress on the plant and allows it to adjust immediately when the new season starts. Try to avoid doing any major work during the growing season, since this can stress the plant and lead to problems with surrounding plants.

Most of the work we do each season centers around thinning. If a plant is allowed to become overly thick and unruly, it will often not display its best qualities in bloom, foliage, or structure. When thinning, look for crossing limbs and try to balance the look of the overall plant by removing some of the more severe crosses. As a rule of thumb, start by cutting smaller branches and become more aggressive

We cut our plant of *Salix alba* var. *vitellina* 'Britzensis' to 2–3 feet (0.6–0.9 m) in early spring to ensure brilliantly colored stems in winter. Though it looks rough at this point, it quickly recovers and ultimately grows to 6–8 feet (1.8 m to 2.4 m) tall.

as needed and as you become more comfortable. Thinning also allows more light into the understory, giving smaller plants a much better chance to thrive.

Stooling

We have increased our use of stooling in the garden, as this can be a valuable tool when used in moderation. Many shrubs are at their best only when they are growing quickly the first few years after they are planted; after this point, they reach their ultimate size and start to degrade. This is particularly true with shrubs grown mainly for their bark color and foliage. One prime example is *Cornus sanguinea* 'Midwinter Fire', a shrubby dogwood with spectacularly colored winter bark but little bloom to speak of. We prune this plant down to about 6–10 inches (15–25 cm) from the ground in spring and see new growth in the area of 4–5 feet (1.2–1.5 m) each growing season. We do this for a couple of reasons: it allows us to maintain the plant at a consistent size, and the best bark color frequently occurs on new growth.

When we suggest stooling to our customers, they often look at us like we just asked them to amputate their own arm. It may be difficult at first to swallow the idea of cutting off a plant you have just purchased, but if you are willing to take the plunge, it can result in some excellent growth habits.

Pollarding

Another technique we sometimes use is pollarding. This act is a little more violent and can be shocking to the senses at times. When you pollard a plant, you take it back to a central structure. It is akin to tearing everything off a skyscraper and leaving just the metal frame. You can pollard many small trees and even some shrubs. It requires work each season, but in the right area it can prove worthwhile.

The drive to our house and office is lined with a row of sycamore trees we have been pollarding since the 1960s. These trees grow 10–12 feet (3–3.6 m) of new branches each season from the massive clubs at the end of each short branch off the main trunk. Some of these clubs are 2 feet (0.6 m) through. In winter they look almost like sculptures, and in summer they look like nicely rounded trees. We get more questions about those trees than anything else. Some people think they are incredibly ugly and wonder why we do it. We like the structure and the shapes they make, especially in winter. We also love the comments and discussions they elicit.

Mulching

Mulching is paramount in the garden for a number of reasons. For us it is mainly about weed control, but there are other equally important reasons to do it. Each season we place roughly 1–2 inches (2.5–5 cm) of finely ground bark dust on the entire garden. This is an expensive and time-consuming process, but the rewards are beyond anything you can imagine. In our area of the country there are hundreds of annual weeds just waiting to take over planting beds. If you allow them to get a foothold, it can become a second job just trying to keep them at bay. We have found that by doing our cleanup and mulching as early as possible in the season, or even in winter, we suppress 90 percent of our annual weeds. The longer you do this, the better the results; it will eventually create an almost sterile environment on the surface, and weeds will have a hard time germinating.

In the older portions of the garden where we have mulched for years, there is little weeding to be done during the growing season. Many people try to use material that is either too coarse or a compost blend that will allow weeds to germinate and grow. If you have access to the finer grinds, try them and see if they work for you; they have made our lives much easier. Check with local suppliers before you order, and look at the options available in your area. Mulching also keeps us from having to fertilize in the garden beds themselves. By adding new material each year and allowing it to break down naturally, we provide a humus layer that helps nurture the plants.

Magnolias blooming in early spring mark the beginning of our growing season. The mulch applied in winter will continue to nurture these garden plants and suppress weeds through the rest of the season.

One recent January, Roger was giving a lecture in Portland, Oregon, and when he suggested to the group that they should be out gardening during this time of year, they broke into uncontrollable laughter. We do the bulk of our gardening maintenance from December through February. While this may seem psychotic to some people, we feel strongly that this one act saves us hundreds of hours during the rest of the year.

We begin by removing all the leaves and raking out all the beds in the last days of December. Once the beds are clean, we complete all our pruning, planting, and redesigning for the year. Then we rake the beds one final time just prior to mulching. The mulching is generally completed in the second week of February, with 1–2 inches (2.5–5 cm) of bark dust blown over the entire garden. This timing allows the perennials to grow up through the new layer and suppresses the growth of weeds for the season.

We realize that in some areas of the country the spring season is extremely short and work isn't possible during winter, but this maintenance can be completed even during a narrow window of time. If you are in an extreme climate, all you can do is work toward this model. Even if you are unable to achieve complete success, you will see positive results and be rewarded for your efforts.

A to Z Plant Directory

Abeliophyllum distichum (white forsythia)
This Korean native was only discovered in the 1920s. We are trying it in several areas to determine the best way to grow it. Although we have seen beautiful specimens, we haven't yet grown the nicest plants in our own garden. *Abeliophyllum distichum* grows 4–6 feet (1.2–1.8 m) tall and has dark green foliage all summer and some yellow fall color. Our plants bloom in late winter, with small white clusters covering the stems. The flowers are usually white tinged with pink and are slightly fragrant. A selection called 'Roseum' has soft pink flowers that hold the pink throughout the bloom season. *Abeliophyllum distichum* seems to do best in full sun with some wind protection to protect the flowers from early frost.

Origin: Korea.

Hardiness: Zones 4–8.

Exposure: Sun.

Opposite: *Deutzia hybrida* 'Magicien'.

Abeliophyllum distichum.

Acer palmatum (Japanese maple)

What would we gardeners do without the Japanese maple to grace our gardens? Throughout much of the United States, *A. palmatum* is a standard landscape plant, whether as a graceful weeping laceleaf form (*A. palmatum* var. *dissectum*) or a more robust, upright-growing tree. There are hundreds if not thousands of Japanese maples to choose from, and wonderful new forms continue to come out of Japan. These can be dwarf plants just 18 inches (45 cm) tall or 40-foot (12 m) trees. The foliage can be green, yellow, purple, or variegated. The bark can be red, green, or yellow and is sometimes corky and fissured. Most Japanese maples get too large to be appropriate for this book, but we include some of the finest smaller selections.

Origin: Japan.
Hardiness: Zones 5–9.
Exposure: Sun to partial shade.

Acer palmatum var. dissectum 'Red Filigree Lace'.

This cascading laceleaf maple has some of the most finely dissected foliage of any *A. palmatum*. It was discovered by nurseryman William Curtis as a seedling and changed hands numerous times over many years until someone could propagate it. Its dark purple foliage has to be seen to be appreciated. The fall color is brilliant red.

Acer palmatum var. dissectum 'Seiryu'.

This 15- to 20-foot (4.6 m to 6 m) laceleaf maple is a small, upright, vase-shaped tree. The medium green leaves are small and dissected like any cascading laceleaf. The fall color can be orange or yellow to deep burgundy red depending on the location.

Acer palmatum 'Fairy Hair'.

Amaze your friends and confuse the plant nerds. Sounds like the old newspaper ads for cottonwoods, doesn't it? 'Fairy Hair' is, however, a very slow growing maple, to perhaps 2 feet (0.6 m) tall after many years. Our five-year-old specimen is 18 inches (45 cm) tall. This introduction from Talon Buchholz will always be scarce because of its slow growth but is worth the search. It has the narrowest leaflets we have seen on any Japanese maple; they are hair-thin and dark purple-green, turning yellow in fall.

Acer palmatum 'Shaina'.

This fine, very slow growing, purple-leaved cultivar appeared as a bud mutation of *A. palmatum* 'Bloodgood'. Greer Gardens near Eugene, Oregon, introduced it in 1988. Our plant is probably fifteen years old and is an upright 4- to 5-foot (1.2 m to 1.5 m) shrub with very congested, rich purple leaves that turn a brilliant red in fall. 'Shaina' is excellent in the garden but very difficult as a container plant. For this reason we have stopped growing it in our nursery but wouldn't be without it in our garden. It is best to plant it as a small specimen.

Acer palmatum 'Shishigashira' (lion's mane maple).

This unusual cultivar grows to 20 feet

Opposite top: *Acer palmatum* 'Shaina'.

Opposite bottom: *Acer palmatum* 'Shishigashira' in fall.

(6 m) tall after thirty or forty years. The leaves are dark green with crinkled edges and turn pumpkin orange. The tufted foliage is slow but can grow quickly for a year and then return to the bunched form. We grow 'Shishigashira' with *Cornus sanguinea* 'Midwinter Fire'; the dogwood's yellow fall color combines well with the orange-yellow maple.

Acer palmatum 'Ukigumo' (floating clouds maple). An excellent woodland garden plant that will brighten a shady area. Our plant is twenty years old and only 7–8 feet (2.1–2.4 m) tall. The foliage is dark green with white overlay, with the overall effect of a small white tree. When the plant is young, the foliage is green with a few spots, but as the tree ages it changes to mostly white. Don't overfertilize, as this cultivar will grow fast and be just a green-leaved *A. palmatum*.

Aralia elata (devil's walking stick)
The common name refers to the thorns on this plant's stems and leaves. The stems are sparingly branched and very upright, to perhaps 15–18 feet (4.6–5.5 m). This running shrub has many trunks coming out of the ground. We have seen old plants in lawns that actually form an 8-inch (20 cm) trunk, but most plants are thickets. Don't plant *A. elata* in areas with good soil and moisture, as it can be aggressive, but do try this handsome shrub if you have the space. Its pinnate leaves, up to 3 feet (0.9 m) long, are held at the top of the branches, creating a tropical effect, though *A. elata* is very hardy. The flowers are at the ends of the branches in late summer, held in huge clusters that can be 18 inches (45 cm) across. The individual small, white flowers attract lots of different bees and insects. We have seen and grown four cultivars, all of which are expensive and difficult to find but well worth it.

Origin: Japan, Korea.
Hardiness: Zones 4–8.
Exposure: Sun to partial shade.

Aralia elata 'Aureovariegata'. Among the finest of any variegated shrubs we grow. In spring the large, pinnate leaves have a broad yellow margin, which by midsummer is more creamy white. Seems to be easier to grow than *A. elata* 'Variegata'.

Aralia elata 'Golden Umbrella'. The leaves hold their yellow color through the whole summer. We saw a plant at Heronswood Nursery in Kingston, Washington, and were stunned. Now to just find a plant!

Aralia elata 'Silver Umbrella'. Our tree is 20 feet (6 m) tall and has smaller leaves and thinner white margins than 'Aureovariegata' and 'Golden Umbrella'. Overall, a much more subtle variegation and plant. 'Silver Umbrella' seems to get bigger than all the other forms of *A. elata*.

Opposite: *Aralia elata* 'Aureovariegata' growing with *Kniphofia* and *Phygelius*.

Opposite: The small, subtle leaves of *Aralia elata* 'Silver Umbrella' provide a delicate backdrop for summer flowers.

Aralia elata 'Variegata'. A stunning, broad, cream-variegated form. The 2- to 3-foot (0.6 m to 0.9 m) leaves will light up any woodland garden all summer. The flowers are in 18-inch (45 cm) clusters in late summer.

Arbutus unedo (strawberry tree)

This attractive evergreen should be planted in gardens more often. It is hardy to perhaps 5°F (–15°C) and in our garden has only been killed once, at –12°F (–24°C). A large shrub or small tree, it grows in full sun or semi-shade and is especially nice in the coastal Pacific Northwest or California. It can withstand both hot and cool climates. The dark green, serrate leaves are 3 inches (7.5 cm) long and ¾ inch (1.9 cm) wide. *Arbutus unedo* has fissured bark and stems that curve attractively. The flowers are small white urns that appear from late summer to early winter, coinciding with the appearance of the round red fruit. This shrub looks great through fall

Aralia elata 'Variegata' will brighten any woodland garden.

and winter and is beautiful in Christmas arrangements.

Origin: Ireland to the Mediterranean.
Hardiness: Zones 7–9.
Exposure: Sun.

Arbutus unedo 'Elfin King'. A much smaller shrubby form to 6–8 feet (1.8–2.4 m) tall that still has the attractive flowers and fruit. We have seen other forms in books but haven't seen them available in the United States.

Aucuba japonica 'Rozannie'

Several varieties of *Aucuba* are available, but many are spotted or blotched and put into dark, awful places where few other shrubs will grow. We grow 'Rozannie' for its evergreen foliage on a compact plant to 4 feet (1.2 m) tall. The dark green leaves almost glow with glossiness. Our plants have endured temperatures below 0°F (–18°C) several times and were not hurt at all. The flowers are insignificant, but the fruits are about 1 inch (2.5 cm) across and rich red. 'Rozannie' is said to be self-fertile, but until we added more aucubas of other cultivars, it didn't produce any fruit. Even without the fruit, this form is very attractive.

Origin: Japan.
Hardiness: Zones 6–10.
Exposure: Shade.

Azara microphylla

A group of South American shrubs or small trees for the mild garden. *Azara microphylla* is the most commonly grown species in West Coast gardens. Our plants were cut to the ground by temperatures as low as 0°F (–18°C) but came back quickly. This species is an upright grower to 15 feet (4.6 m). The evergreen leaves are tiny, perhaps 1/2 inch (1.25 cm) by 1/4 inch (0.6 cm) wide. The branches grow as flattened, open groups of stems. An attractive tree for a small landscape in semishade. The flowers are small golden puffs with a vanilla scent in late winter to early spring.

Origin: Chile.
Hardiness: Zones 7–9.
Exposure: Shade.

Azara microphylla 'Variegata'. This cultivar is the same size as the species but has wide, creamy yellow foliage that makes it a showier plant.

Berberis (barberry)

Barberries are among the most beautiful plants we grow, and without them our garden would be much duller year-round. We realize that these shrubs have faults—*B. thunbergii*, for example, self-seeds in the northeastern United States. The thorns are also a drawback to many gardeners. In fact we stayed away from barberries for years because of the thorns. If given their space, however, these plants need little pruning and little care, so you won't be exposed to the thorns on a regular basis. The evergreen barberries have excellent glossy foliage and seem to be more tender than the *B. thunbergii* cultivars. Many barberries have pink, black, or red fruit in fall and can be striking for a long period of time.

Origin: Asia, South America.
Hardiness: Zones 6–10.
Exposure: Sun to partial shade.

In winter some leaves of *Berberis calliantha* turn red-orange.

Berberis calliantha. This evergreen species from Tibet reaches 2–3 feet (0.6–0.9 m) tall. It is irregular in form and wider than tall. Our plant has some suckers but isn't invasive. The convex, dark green leaves are very glossy on top and white underneath, creating a great contrast. In winter some of the old leaves turn rich red-orange, making another show. In midspring the flowers, ½ inch (1.25 cm) wide, are like little yellow daffodils. This species would do well on top of a low wall. Hardy in zones 6–9. Grow in sun to partial shade.

Berberis darwinii. Why isn't this gorgeous Chilean shrub grown more often? It was seen regularly in the 1950s and 1960s, but fashions change. From the 1970s to the 1990s, orange seemed to be out as most gardeners wanted only pastels. (How dull.) *Berberis darwinii* gets to be 8 feet (2.4 m) tall and 8 feet wide in perhaps twenty years. It is thickly covered with small, dark green leaves and makes an excellent background for other perennials and shrubs. The flowers appear in early spring and are small but very heavily produced. Their light orange is the perfect complement to the dark foliage. In fall our

Berberis darwinii.

plants have many dark purple-blue fruits. This fine evergreen plant is hardy in zones 6–10. Grow in sun.

Berberis replicata. We discovered this great plant at Western Hills Nursery in Occidental, California. We can't find much information about it, but it is one of the most beautiful evergreens in our garden. Reaching 8–10 feet (2.4–3 m) tall, it makes a fine individual shrub or large screen or hedge. The dark green leaves are 2 inches (5 cm) long and ½ inch (1.25 cm) wide. During spring and summer the new growth is rich purple, creating a more beautiful display than the small yellow flowers. Grow in sun to partial shade.

Berberis thunbergii. A large group of deciduous barberry selections from Japan, hardy in zones 4–8. These are not suggested for the Northeast because of their tendency to seed profusely and invade wild areas, but in other parts of the country they are superb shrubs with many uses. Since the 1980s a great range of plant types have been available, from narrow, golden dwarf, and purple dwarf forms to plants with huge purple foliage. Cultivars come in a range of sizes—and why should we shear plants into balls or boxes to keep them a certain size when barberries will grow exactly the size we want? Grow in sun.

The dark purple foliage of *Berberis thunbergii* f. *atropurpurea* 'Helmond Pillar' stands out in any garden.

***Berberis thunbergii* f. *atropurpurea* 'Helmond Pillar'.** When we first saw pictures of this plant in the late 1970s, we wanted it at once. We were given a plant from Hollandia Gardens Nursery in Seattle, and after more than twenty-five years it reached 6 feet (1.8 m) tall and 2 feet (0.6 m) wide. The dark purple foliage holds its color all summer. Our plants need a light pruning once a year. We have also seen people use fishing line to make their plants narrower. We prefer the looser form for our garden.

Berberis thunbergii 'Bagatelle'.

Berberis thunbergii 'Bagatelle'. This handsomely colored barberry only reaches 18 inches (45 cm) tall after fifteen years. Young plants are rounded and have reddish new growth followed by rich purple leaves that turn brilliant red in fall. This is a great plant for the rock garden or front of the border. The flowers are very small, as they are with all *B. thunbergii* cultivars.

Berberis thunbergii 'Concorde'. This introduction from Wavecrest Nursery in Michigan is one of the best *B. thunbergii* cultivars we grow. Our plants are irregular shrubs to perhaps 18 inches (45 cm) tall and 18 inches across. The velvety foliage is purple with a dusty grayish cast, turning a gorgeous red in fall. This makes an excellent border shrub, and its dusty purple foliage contrasts well with conifers.

Berberis thunbergii 'Gold Nugget'. This fine golden cultivar is orange-yellow as it leafs out and bright golden yellow all summer. Its habit and size are similar to *B. thunbergii* 'Bagatelle', and it is said to be more sun tolerant than *B. thunbergii* 'Aurea'.

Berberis thunbergii 'Royal Cloak'. This excellent barberry is the giant of the *B. thunbergii* cultivars. "Giant" is relative, however: our plant is 10 feet (3 m) tall and 10 feet wide. 'Royal Cloak' looks like a dark, small-foliaged *Cotinus*. The dark purple leaves make a striking background for perennials or smaller shrubs.

Buxus sempervirens

This plant is almost too well known to need a description, but we will provide one anyway. It can be a tiny dwarf of 6 inches (15 cm) after twenty years or an upright shrub to 10 feet (3 m) tall. All the nondwarf forms can be easily sheared into various shapes. The small, glossy, evergreen leaves can be deep green or variegated.

    Origin: Europe.

    Hardiness: Zones 5–9.

    Exposure: Sun to partial shade.

Buxus sempervirens 'Graham Blandy'. When we first started growing this boxwood we were frustrated by its limbs, which would splay out. It was supposed to be columnar but we found it irregular looking. When we got the plant in the ground, however, it tightened up to make a strong, columnar form 6 feet (1.8 m) tall and 1 foot (0.3 m) across. We do some moderate pruning to keep this selection narrow. It seems to do best with afternoon shade to keep the foliage dark green. Hardy in zones 6–9.

Buxus sempervirens 'Variegata'. We have seen this selection grown as 8- to 10-foot (2.4 m to 3 m) upright shrubs, but our plants are 3–4 feet (0.9–1.2 m) tall and 2 feet (0.6 m) wide with some pruning for flower arrangements. We grow 'Variegata' in either full sun or semishade. It is very attractive for its leaves, with their wide band of cream and dark evergreen centers. Our neighbor's plant has endured –12°F (–24°C) without any damage.

Callicarpa bodinieri var. giraldii
'Profusion'

Over the years we have tried *C. dichotoma*, *C. americana*, and several Chinese species, but these plants are very tender and haven't produced fruit. Our summer nights are cool and our springs are long, so the wood doesn't ripen on *Callicarpa* species in our garden. *Callicarpa bodinieri* var. *giraldii* 'Profusion' is the only cultivar that has fruited consistently

Callicarpa bodinieri var. *giraldii* 'Profusion' in fruit.

Callicarpa bodinieri var. *giraldii* 'Profusion'.

and proven hardy for us. In early summer, small purple flowers appear at the axils of the stems on this 8- to 10-foot (2.4 m to 3 m) shrub. In early fall the small purple fruit occurs in clusters along the stems. Frequently in fall the foliage turns from dark green to gold-pink. The fruit holds on until Christmas or later. The only maintenance we do is to prune out old fruiting wood in spring to reinvigorate the shrub. For its fall fruit color, this has remained among our favorite shrubs for the last thirty years.

Origin: China.

Hardiness: Zones 5–8.

Exposure: Sun.

Calycanthus chinensis (syn. *Sinocalycanthus chinensis*)

This species was first brought to the United States in the 1980s, and we first saw it at Heronswood Nursery in Kingston, Washington. It is a vigorous, open shrub that eventually gets to 15–20 feet (4.6–6 m) tall and probably 10–12 feet (3–3.6 m) wide. The stems can grow really fast on a young plant. The internodes can be over 1 foot (0.3

m) long, making it difficult to create cuttings for propagation. The oval leaves, up to 8 inches (20 cm) long and 3 inches (7.5 cm) wide, are deep green throughout summer, turning butter yellow in fall before dropping. The nodding flowers are white but can be light pink when they open, depending on temperature; they are 2–3 inches (5–7.5 cm) wide and have smaller inner petals that are light yellow surrounded by white outer petals. The flowers appear in late spring and last for about a month. Because they bloom only sporadically, the overall show isn't overwhelming, but the individual flowers are beautiful and are presented on the plant in an attractive way.

Origin: China.
Hardiness: Zones 5–9.
Exposure: Partial shade.

Calycanthus ×raulstonii 'Hartlage Wine'
(syn. ×*Sinocalycalycanthus raulstonii* 'Hartlage Wine')

In the 1980s, one of the first specimens of *C. chinensis* bloomed at the North Carolina State University Arboretum in Raleigh, North Carolina. As one of J. C. Raulston's students, Richard Hartlage crossed *C. chinensis* with *C. floridus*, resulting in a very beautiful plant now known as *C. ×raulstonii* 'Hartlage Wine'. It is larger than *C. floridus* and has larger leaves than our American native.

Calycanthus chinensis.

Calycanthus ×raulstonii 'Hartlage Wine'.

Calycanthus ×*raulstonii* 'Hartlage Wine' has a huge amount of flowers, which are 1½ inches (4 cm) wide and a rich purple-pink. We have seen 1-foot (0.3 m) plants with twenty-five flowers. The flowers appear in late spring, and the bloom season is about a month long. Our plant is in full sun all day, but it will also grow in semishade. We believe 'Hartlage Wine' will be a good plant for our climate as well as the Southeast and many other areas.

> Origin: China (*C. chinensis*), United States (*C. floridus*).
> Hardiness: Zones 5–9.
> Exposure: Sun to partial shade.

Calycanthus 'Venus' (syn. ×*Sinocalycalycanthus* 'Venus')

This hybrid created by Tom Rainey of North Carolina looks like *C.* ×*raulstonii* 'Hartlage Wine', but the flowers are white and more starlike when in bloom, somewhat resembling the flowers of *Magnolia stellata* because the petals are narrow and have some pink at the base. We haven't seen any of the other hybrids in Rainey's program but have heard good things about these fine plants. For now we can add 'Venus' to the list of calycanthus that should be grown more often.

> Origin: China (*C. chinensis*), United States (*C. floridus*).
> Hardiness: Zones 5–9.
> Exposure: Sun to partial shade.

Camellia

These ornamental shrubs have been grown in their native lands for hundreds of years by gardeners, and they have been grown in Western gardens for at least 150 years. The glossy, dark green leaves of *C. japonica* are a standard feature in gardens of the Pacific Coast and in the South from Virginia to Texas. The flowers can be single, semidouble, or formal double, ranging in color from white to pink to deep red, with many hundreds of variations. Our problem in the Northwest is that the flowers can be blemished or ruined when they bloom in early spring. We have tried many forms of *C. japonica* in our garden over the years, but our climate is too cool, and the flowers are ruined most years by rain and cold weather. However, we really like some of the hardier species' first-generation hybrids and *C.* ×*williamsii* hybrids.

Camellia includes an enormous range of options. We strongly encourage you to try the species and newer hardy hybrids from the eastern United States to see what will grow in your garden.

> Origin: China, Japan.
> Hardiness: Zones 6–9.
> Exposure: Afternoon shade.

***Camellia* 'Baby Bear'.** This dwarf (4-foot [1.2 m]) cross between *C. rosaeflora* and *C. tsai* has small, dark green foliage and small, soft pink flowers in midspring. Makes a great container plant that always draws attention. Grow in partial shade.

***Camellia* 'Black Opal'.** We can't find much information on this lovely plant, but we like it for its deep green, narrow leaves with serrated edges. Our plant is 3 feet (0.9 m) tall after ten years. The flowers are like open bells

Camellia 'Black Opal'.

of the deepest maroon in midspring. This is one of the most unusual camellias we've seen. Grow in partial shade.

Camellia japonica 'Bob's Tinsie'. One of the few forms of *C. japonica* that does well in our garden. The glossy foliage and upright habit form a nice backdrop for the rich red, anemone-like flowers. The centers of the flowers have large white stamens. Grow in partial shade to full sun.

Camellia japonica 'Kujaku-tsubaki' (peacock camellia, weeping camellia). This form grows up to 6 feet (1.8 m) tall. The leaves are narrow and slightly twisted on semipendulous stems. Medium red, white-flecked, tubular flowers hang from the plant like Christmas ornaments. This shrub is probably hardy enough to be grown outside in our climate, but we have always used it as a container plant. There is a superb specimen in downtown Ashland, Oregon, that is 7–8 feet (2.1–2.4 m) tall. Grow in partial shade.

Camellia sasanqua. We like the idea of this species, which offers flowers from fall to winter in various shades from white to red. It can be very attractive in the right place. However, all the specimens we have tried to grow have been hit by frosts in fall and frequently hurt or killed in the process. To protect camellias from heavy frosts, many gardeners put them under eves or in shady corners, but *C. sasanqua* tends to look grungy and dusty in these positions. It would be preferable to try this species in slightly milder climes and in areas with reasonable water and air movement. It is hardy in zones 7–9. Grow in sun to shade.

***Camellia* 'Unryu'.** This camellia has foliage and an upright habit like *C. japonica*, but the growth is totally different. Its stems twist at a forty-five-degree angle and are shown to best advantage when pruned lightly. With its contorted stems, dark green leaves, and red bell-like flowers, 'Unryu' makes a good container plant or garden plant. Grow it in sun to partial shade.

***Camellia ×williamsii* 'Brigadoon'.** Similar to *C. ×williamsii* 'Donation' but with larger, more oval foliage. The flowers are also a much deeper pink and more ruffled. Grow in partial shade.

***Camellia ×williamsii* 'Donation'.** This seems to be the finest camellia for the Pacific Northwest. The flowers bloom from late winter to midspring. The buds are of various sizes, but if the flowers are hit by frost the later buds continue to open (if the frost doesn't go below about 25°F [–4°C]). Our original plant is full but not overwhelmed with foliage like *C. japonica*. The leaves are much more narrow and dark matte green. Our plant has all-day sun and amazingly hasn't suffered any sun scald. The flowers are light pink with darker

Camellia ×williamsii 'Donation'.

pink veins in a semidouble form. Grow in sun to partial shade.

Carpenteria californica (California bush poppy)

We first saw this species in Molly Grothaus's Portland garden in the early 1980s. It can grow up to 12 feet (3.6 m) tall though usually reaches 6–8 feet (1.8–2.4 m). The older branches exfoliate to creamy tan, and the evergreen leaves are 4 inches (10 cm) long and ½ inch (1.25 cm) wide. *Carpenteria californica* is related to *Philadelphus* and has 2-inch (5 cm), white, mock orange–like flowers with yellow stamens. They have no scent, but

that is a small price to pay for their beauty. This species grows best in well-drained soil in full sun. Once established (one year), it needs little water during summer in the Pacific Northwest. We grow our plants with rhododendrons; they have similar-looking foliage but also offer early-summer blooms.

Origin: California.
Hardiness: Zones 7–9.
Exposure: Sun.

Carpenteria californica 'Barbara'.

Named for our long-time friend Barbara Coe, gardener, nurserywoman, and expert on California natives, this cultivar has beautiful semidouble

Carpenteria californica 'Barbara'.

Carpenteria californica 'Elizabeth'.

flowers that are frilled, making them fuller looking than those of *C. californica* 'Elizabeth'. 'Barbara' is rarely grown, and we hope this book will encourage more gardeners to grow it. Plant in sun.

Carpenteria californica 'Elizabeth'. Named for Elizabeth McClintock of the University of California, a wonderful writer on magnolias, hydrangeas, and many other plants for *Pacific Horticulture* magazine. This cultivar came from the wild and was grown for its multiple white flowers in a large truss. It

has become the standard *Carpenteria* in the Pacific Northwest and California. Seedlings are rarely grown commercially now because of the difficulty of sprouting the seed. Grow in sun.

Chaenomeles (flowering quince)
These old-fashioned plants appear in mature gardens throughout the temperate world; we regularly see them in old farmyards in the Pacific Northwest. Quinces can be suckering shrubs with many stems coming out of the ground, and many selections can get to 6–8

feet (1.8–2.4 m) tall. The plants we grow are much smaller and much easier to grow and maintain in the garden.

Origin: China.
Hardiness: Zones 5–8.
Exposure: Sun.

Chaenomeles 'Hime'. A superb selection with flowers a combination of brick red and orange. The 3- to 4-foot (0.9 m to 1.2 m) shrub is much lighter in texture than most quinces.

The foliage is small, dark green, and oval. The best part of 'Hime' is its total lack of thorns, which makes it a much better garden shrub. Just don't plant it with any pink flowers close by, as we did—the effect is really jarring. Grow in sun.

Chaenomeles* ×*superba 'Cameo'. A 3- to 4-foot (0.9 m to 1.2 m) spring-blooming shrub. The double flowers are a lovely peachy color and 2 inches (5 cm) across in early spring.

Chaenomeles 'Hime'.

Chaenomeles ×superba 'Hollandia'.

The thorns are a problem mainly during handling in the nursery and during planting (providing 'Cameo' isn't grown under a broad-leaved deciduous tree, in which case it will be tricky picking out the leaves that fall into the thorny quince). Grow in full sun to get the best flowering.

Chaenomeles ×superba 'Hollandia'. This outstanding winter- to spring-blooming (sometimes summer-blooming) shrub has the most brilliant red flowers imaginable. Our plant flowers from late fall until midspring, continuing sporadically until early fall. The 2-inch (5 cm) red flowers have golden yel-

low stamens. We follow Jane Platt's excellent idea of growing our plant against a fence; the flowers are easy to see and are best shown off with just a small amount of pruning each year. Grow in sun.

Chimonanthus praecox (wintersweet)
Discovered in China in the 1760s, this wonderful plant for the winter garden spreads its fragrance at least 100 feet (30 m). It is an open shrub up to 12 feet (3.6 m) tall and 6–8 feet (1.8–2.4 m) wide. The deciduous leaves are narrow and medium green, with a sandpaper texture. Although it has a glorious fragrance, *C. praecox* isn't as showy as many winter- or

early spring–flowering shrubs. Small yellow flowers with purple petals at their centers appear in midwinter. During summer there is little reason to grow this species, but it makes a good structure for clematis.

    Origin: China.
    Hardiness: Zones 7–9.
    Exposure: Sun to afternoon shade.

Chimonanthus praecox 'Luteus'. This cultivar is the same size as the species and has the same flower size and foliage, but its flowers are a beautiful golden yellow and very fragrant. We have heard that the fragrance isn't as strong as the species, but we disagree: if anything, it is stronger. 'Luteus' seems to do best in full sun with some protection from winter winds.

Chionanthus (fringe tree)

This small genus from China and the eastern United States belongs to the olive family. We have grown these fine shrubs since the 1980s and are always impressed with their beautiful foliage and flowers. These easy-growing, large shrubs are excellent for different climates, with *C. retusus* doing best in warmer climates and *C. virginicus* thriving in cooler areas. The foliage is very different between these species, but their flowers are similar, though larger in *C. virginicus*. In warm climates like the South and California, *C. retusus* is spectacular in late spring when it is covered with white flowers. Unfortunately, the moderate summers of our own climate prevent *C. retusus* from producing any flowers, so we don't recommend this species for the Pacific Northwest or Britain.

    Origin: United States from Texas to Pennsylvania and New Jersey.
    Hardiness: Zones 4–9.
    Exposure: Sun.

Chionanthus virginicus. This large shrub gets to 18 feet (5.5 m) tall and 12 feet (3.6 m) across in twenty-five years. Our plant has four or five major trunks, but we have seen plants with a single stem (small tree). The

The scented white flowers of *Chionanthus virginicus*.

gray-tan bark makes a nice backdrop for the deep green leaves. *Chionanthus virginicus* is absolutely the last of any deciduous shrub to leaf out. (On that note, don't dig it up when it lacks foliage in April and May.) Fragrant white flowers appear in late spring and cover the shrub like thousands of silk shreds. The leaves aren't mature at bloom time, so the flowers make an amazing display. Female plants can have olivelike fruits from late summer into fall. Even though *C. virginicus* is a member of the olive family, it is very hardy to at least –20°F (–29°C). An excellent plant for its beautiful white flowers, dark green foliage, and attractive yellow fall color. Grow in sun to partial shade.

Chionanthus virginicus in summer.

Opposite: *Chionanthus virginicus* in fall.

Choisya ternata (Mexican orange)
An old standard landscape plant in the West. The dark evergreen leaves are glossy and fully cover this 5- to 6-foot (1.5 m to 1.8 m) plant. White flowers appear in midspring, but our plant blooms sporadically through the year. The flowers are orange-scented, hence the common name. This species has survived –12°F (–24°C) in our area.

    Origin: Mexico.
    Hardiness: Zones 7–9.
    Exposure: Partial shade.

Choisya ternata 'Aztec Pearl'. The very narrow leaflets of this English hybrid are deep forest green. Our plant is 6–7 feet (1.8–2.1 m) tall and filters through other shrubs. The flowers are white and sweetly citrus-scented in spring. Grow in partial shade.

Choisya ternata 'Sundance'. Named in 1986, this fine evergreen selection from Peter Catt of Liss Forest Nursery, England, came to us through the plant nerd circle. It has rich golden yellow foliage. Its white, fragrant flowers are identical to those of the species.

Opposite top: The white, scented flowers and narrow, deep green leaflets of *Choisya ternata* 'Aztec Pearl'.

Opposite bottom: The golden foliage and white flowers of *Choisya ternata* 'Sundance'.

Choisya ternata 'Aztec Pearl'.

We grow 'Sundance' in sites with morning sun, afternoon shade, or filtered shade.

Clethra alnifolia (summersweet)

This native of the southeastern United States can grow up to 8 feet (2.4 m) tall in time, though most cultivars grow to 3–6 feet (0.9–1.8 m). It is a slowly spreading, suckering shrub. The dark green leaves are 3 inches (7.5 cm) long and 1/2 inch (1.25 cm) wide and in fall turn a beautiful clear yellow. The flowers, which are borne in upright panicles in mid to late summer, can be creamy white to rich pink and are very fragrant. The flower heads provide year-round interest, turning a rich brown in fall and holding on through winter. We find that *C. alnifolia* selections are very easy to grow.

> Origin: Southeastern United States.
> Hardiness: Zones 4–9.
> Exposure: Sun to light shade.

Clethra alnifolia 'Hummingbird'. The great plantsman Fred Galle named this cultivar for Hummingbird Lake at Callaway Gardens in Pine Mountain, Georgia, where he was director of horticulture. This low grower to 2–3 feet (0.6–0.9 m) makes an excellent spreader in full sun or semishade. It is an excellent alternative to the insanely big plants (forsythia, barberries) so often butchered into square or round shapes in our landscapes.

Clethra alnifolia 'Ruby Spice'. Discovered at Broken Arrow Nursery in Hamden, Connecticut. We used to grow *C. alnifolia* 'Pink Spire', but the rich pink inflorescences of 'Ruby Spice' are a much deeper color. The flowers appear in midsummer, and the pink holds up in temperatures of 90°F–100°F (32°C–38°C). The fall color is bright golden yellow and makes a pretty foil for the dark brown seed pods. Grow in sun to partial shade.

Clethra alnifolia 'September Beauty'. This plant blooms later in the summer than any other *Clethra* cultivar, with panicles of white flowers 3–4 inches (7.5–10 cm) long. Grow in sun to partial shade.

Clethra barbinervis

A Japanese species that grows to the size of a small tree, 20–25 feet (6–7.6 m). The plant we grow came from Jane Platt in the early 1980s and is much slower growing and more handsome than the species. Our original plant is 6 feet (1.8 m) tall and 5–6 feet (1.5–1.8 m) wide, with foliage that is deep green all summer, turning an attractive orange and yellow in fall. Jane's form blooms in early summer, its drooping panicles of white flowers lovely against the dark green foliage. The bark eventually exfoliates like that of *Stewartia pseudocamellia*. Jane's original plant had lovely bark, but ours has yet to exfoliate.

> Origin: Japan.
> Hardiness: Zones 6–9.
> Exposure: Sun to partial shade.

Opposite top: *Clethra barbinervis* in summer.

Opposite bottom: *Clethra barbinervis* in fall.

Comptonia peregrina

This underused, ultrahardy native found from Canada to North Carolina is a suckering shrub for dry, gravelly soils. We grow it in well-watered (but well-draining), rich soil, and it forms attractive, mounded shrubs 2–4 feet (0.6–1.2 m) tall. The narrow leaves are 4 inches (10 cm) long and ½ inch (1.25 cm) wide. The sweetly scented, pinnate leaves are dark green in summer, turning yellow, russet, and brown in fall. The female catkins are tiny red brushes, and the small (1 inch [2.5 cm]) male catkins appear in early spring at the ends of the branches. This plant is difficult to propagate but is a handsome shrub and can be used for fragrant bouquets.

Origin: Eastern United States.

Hardiness: Zones 2–8.

Exposure: Sun.

Cornus (dogwood)

Dogwoods are such a staple throughout the American landscape that we can all remember a favorite tree, whether from our own or a friend's garden, or from the wild, where these trees occur in glorious drifts. For the purposes of this book, we focus not on the tree forms but on their smaller, shrubby cousins. These are mostly multistemmed, bushy plants 10–20 feet (3–6 m) tall. Many have brilliant red, orange, or yellow winter stems. The foliage is narrow and fine textured during summer. Some varieties are variegated or have good fall color. All have terminal panicles of flowers and are without bracts. Many of these adaptable plants can grow in both wet areas and well-drained areas. In all, the dogwoods we present have showy stems and foliage well suited for any garden.

Origin: Northern Hemisphere.

Hardiness: Zones 4–9.

Exposure: Sun.

Cornus alternifolia 'Argentea'. "Stunning" is the word that comes to mind when you see this selection from the eastern United States. At The Garden House in Devon, England, we were overwhelmed to see twenty-five to thirty plants of 'Argentea' grown as drifts. In the United States this plant gets 12–15 feet (3.6–4.6 m) tall and 8–10 feet (20–25

Below: The stunning structure and foliage of *Cornus alternifolia* 'Argentea'.

Opposite: 'Variegata', by comparison, is too large to be considered a shrub. *Cornus alternifolia* 'Argentea' offers a similar effect in a smaller size.

cm) across. Those we have seen have up-right trunks and horizontal side branches, creating a lovely layered form similar to *C. controversa* 'Variegata' (wedding cake tree). The leaves, which are much smaller and narrower than 'Variegata', are light green with a narrow ivory margin. The flowers are small and have no bracts but are followed by black fruit in fall. Grow 'Argentea' in sun, but provide afternoon shade in warm climates. Our plants don't burn in full sun but bleach out by midsummer. 'Argentea' is one of the finest variegated shrubs that can be grown in our gardens. Even the smallest landscapes have room for this plant, with its attractive structure, dark purple winter stems, and beautiful summer foliage. Hardy in zones 4–9.

Cornus sanguinea 'Compressa'. Native to Europe, *C. sanguinea* resembles *C. alba* with much smaller stems, and like *C. alba*, it grows as a suckering shrub. The species itself is not a great shrub, but 'Compressa' is an unusual oddity that can be used with great success in the garden. We have seen it reach up to 6 feet (1.8 m) tall and 1 foot (0.3 m) wide. It is a columnar plant completely covered with deep green foliage. The leaves are plastered one on top of another, creating a congested form. The purple-yellow fall color is followed by purple winter stems. Our plant has yet to flower or fruit, but it makes a perfect broad-leaved exclamation point in the garden. Hardy in zones 4–9. Grow in sun.

Cornus sanguinea 'Midwinter Fire'. Another *C. sanguinea* cultivar of great garden merit. Left to its own devices, this dogwood can get to 12–15 feet (3.6–4.6 m) tall with bright red-yellow new growth. We, however, grow 'Midwinter Fire' as a suckering perennial to 4–5 feet (1.2–1.5 m) tall, cutting down our plants in early spring just before they begin to bud and grow. You can do this by cutting the plant to about 6–8 inches (15–20 cm) tall. No need to be too careful, as you would with a rose—just get it right down. The stems begin red at ground level and change to orange and yellow. We grow some of our plants with *Choisya ternata* 'Sundance', which has bright yellow, evergreen foliage, and also grow 'Midwinter Fire' along our driveway, where the plants positively glow when lit up

Cornus sanguinea 'Midwinter Fire' in fall, with golden leaves.

The stems of *Cornus sanguinea* 'Midwinter Fire' are bright red, orange, and yellow.

by headlights. New cultivars from Holland promise even brighter orange, red, yellow, or brilliant green stems. Hardy in zones 4–9. Grow in sun.

Cornus sericea 'Hedgrows Gold'. This selection of our native stream dogwood was named and introduced by our friends David Mason and Susie Grimm of Hedgerows Nurs-

ery in McMinnville, Oregon. It can reach 10–12 feet (3–3.6 m) tall and forms a thicket of deep red stems. We cut our plants down to 18 inches (45 cm) each year so that they grow to just 6 feet (1.8 m) tall. They offer excellent variegation. In spring the leaves emerge with medium green centers and attractive golden yellow margins, and the variegation lasts through most of the summer. 'Hedgrows

Opposite: *Cornus sericea* 'Hedgrows Gold'.

Gold' is probably the finest of the golden-variegated shrubby dogwoods. Hardy in zones 5–9. Grow in sun.

Corokia cotoneaster (wire-netting bush)

This shrub is fascinating for its texture. The common name refers to its unusual, black, contorted stems and tiny, dark green leaves. The foliage is so small that the stems become the main reason to grow the plant. Our plant is 5–6 feet (1.5–1.8 m) tall in the ground but can make a conversation piece in a large container. The flowers appear in spring and are small, bright yellow stars among the black stems. Many books describe the flowers as sparse, but in our climate they are quite striking.

    Origin: New Zealand.
    Hardiness: Zones 7–10.
    Exposure: Sun.

Corylopsis

A group of fine shrubs for the woodland garden. Corylopsis are Asian members of the witch hazel family, Hamamelidaceae. Depending on the variety, these shrubs can be 5–6 feet (1.5–1.8 m) all the way up to 15–18 feet (4.6–5.5 m) tall. They have an open, irregular branching habit. The main stems do not get nearly as large as those of *Hamamelis*, giving corylopsis a lighter, more graceful structure. Their flowers are all yellow, with racemes that vary in length and width. We have been growing these shrubs since the 1970s and are more impressed every year with their winter grace, yellow spring flowers, and handsome yellow fall foliage.

    Origin: Japan, China.
    Hardiness: Zones 7–8.
    Exposure: Partial shade to sun.

Corylopsis pauciflora. This Japanese native is by far the finest *Corylopsis* species for modern gardens. Our plants are 6 feet (1.8 m) tall and 6–7 feet (1.8–2.1 m) across after twenty-five years; some are on a southeast-facing berm

The yellow flowers of *Corylopsis pauciflora* herald spring, paired here with the white flowers of *Magnolia ×loebneri* 'Merrill'.

where they thrive in full sun. The stems are very fine, so in winter the plant structure is beautiful even though the stems are not brightly colored. The leaves are 1½ inches (4 cm) long and oval, with a purple vein along the edge during spring; in fall they turn a beautiful butter yellow. The small yellow flowers are borne in racemes in early spring. These are the smallest flowers of any *Corylopsis* species, but they are profusely borne, very delicate, and make a wonderful show. Hardy in zones 6–8. Grow in sun to partial shade.

Corylopsis sinensis var. **sinensis** 'Spring Purple' (syn. *C. willmottiae* 'Spring Purple'). We recommend this cultivar, which we have grown since the 1980s, because of its narrow, purple spring leaves. It originated in western China but came to us from Hillier Nurseries of Hampshire, United Kingdom, and we like it more the longer we grow it. Our plants are 10 feet (3 m) tall in semishade. Although they were damaged at 0°F (–18°C), they recovered quickly. The flowers have longer racemes than *C. spicata* but are the same soft yellow, and they are quickly followed by the purple leaves. Hardy in zones 7–8. Grow in partial shade.

Corylopsis spicata. This Japanese native is one of the larger *Corylopsis* species, reaching 10–12 feet (3–3.6 m) tall and as wide. The

Opposite: The butter yellow fall foliage of *Corylopsis pauciflora* is striking beside the red leaves of *Stewartia pseudocamellia*.

Corylopsis spicata in spring flower.

foliage is deep green from spring through summer and turns golden yellow by fall. Some years the fall color is excellent; other years it is not. The March flowers are 2 inches (5 cm) long and ½ inch (1.25 cm) wide and seem amazingly hardy in the face of late frosts. *Corylopsis spicata* is similar to several of the larger flowering species of *Corylopsis*. These are variations of plant size, flower size, and foliage, and all seem to be garden-worthy shrubs. *Corylopsis spicata* looks gorgeous with *Lathyrus vernus* and brightly colored *Primula* cultivars at its feet. 'Aurea' is a lovely golden-leaved form that adds color to the garden from spring through fall. Hardy in zones 6–8. Grow in partial shade.

Cotinus (smoke bush)

These large shrubs can grow to over 20 feet (6 m) tall and create some beautiful foliage effects, with green, purple, or yellow leaves in summer. The oval leaves vary in length, from 2–3 inches (5–7.5 cm) in *C. coggygria* to up to 8 inches (20 cm) in *C. obovatus* (native to the southeastern United States). The flowers are clusters of fluffy inflorescences resembling a cloud of smoke. Many gardeners favor this smoke effect, but we prefer the appearance of the foliage, so we prune these shrubs hard in early spring. Larger hybrids like *C.* 'Grace' are pruned down to 6 feet (1.8 m) to retain a framework for the fast new growth. We have tried cutting 'Grace' to 2 feet (0.6 m), but this resulted in a floppy mess of stems. Even starting with a 6-foot (1.8 m) frame, our plants get to 12–14 feet (3.6–4.3 m) each summer. *Cotinus coggygria* cultivars can be pruned to 18 inches (45 cm).

Pruning this way eliminates flowers but results in excellent foliage. Let plants grow one to two years before pruning to be sure they are well rooted.

Origin: Eastern Europe to Asia and America.

Hardiness: Zones 4–8.

Exposure: Sun.

Cotinus coggygria Golden Spirit ('Ancot'). Wow! This golden-foliaged Dutch introduction came on the market in the late 1990s. It was a welcome change from the typical green or purple foliage. Golden Spirit is said to reach only 10–12 feet (3–3.6 m) tall without hard pruning. It took us four or five years to find a plant for our own garden, as we had many missteps before finally locating an American source. The foliage is brilliant golden yellow all summer, turning a softer yellow with pink-purple highlights in fall. Grow in sun.

Cotinus coggygria 'Royal Purple'. Our favorite purple-leaved selection of *C. coggygria*. The 2-inch (5 cm) oval leaves are very dark purple all summer and purple with red highlights in fall. When cut back each year, 'Royal Purple' makes an 8- to 10-foot (2.4 m to 3 m) shrub and is a great background for perennial borders. Grow in sun.

Cotinus 'Grace'. In a word, stunning! A hybrid of *C. coggygria* 'Velvet Cloak' and *C. obovatus* made by Peter Dummer at Hillier Nurseries in the United Kingdom. The leaves are large, 8–10 inches (20–25 cm) long, and oval like *C. obovatus*, but a glowing light purple like

The stunning light purple leaves of *Cotinus* 'Grace'.

In fall the foliage of *Cotinus* 'Grace' turns a glowing pink-red and purple.

C. coggygria. Our plants grow to 12–15 feet (3.6–4.6 m) tall each summer with very hard pruning. If they were allowed to grow naturally, we assume they would reach 25–30 feet (7.6–9 m). If left unpruned, the flower clusters will reach 12 inches (30 cm) across and make a show in mid to late summer. 'Grace' is an inspiring large shrub in fall, when it glows pink-red and purple. Grow in sun.

Crinodendron hookerianum

A plant for very mild areas of the Pacific Coast, from Seattle to the central coast of California. We know of a plant in Lake Oswego, Oregon, that has survived and thrived for twenty years. Since it is a Chilean native, don't try it in the South or East; it won't take the heat and humidity. This upright evergreen shrub has narrow, toothed leaves 2–3 inches (5–7.5 cm) long. We have seen 15- to 20-foot (4.6 m to 6 m) shrubs in coastal Washington. The flowers look like waxy, deep reddish pink strawberries. The thickened petals open partially, so essentially what you see are opening buds. Our garden is too cold for *C. hookerianum* to survive permanently outdoors. However, we always have a plant in a container to show off the fascinating red flowers in early summer. It could be fun to plant *C. hookerianum* in a coolhouse so it could be in the soil with some protection.

Origin: Chile.

Hardiness: Zones 7–9.

Exposure: Partial shade.

Cytisus battandieri (pineapple broom)

Don't be put off this plant because of the genus: pineapple broom is so unlike any broom

The golden flowers of *Cytisus battandieri* are pineapple-scented.

you've ever seen, it will amaze you. It is an upright grower to 20 feet (6 m) with multiple stems. The foliage looks like that of a laburnum, but with tiny silver hairs that make the leaves gray-green from spring to fall. Appearing in early summer, the flowers are also similar to laburnums (to which *Cytisus* is related and to which it is frequently grafted) but more golden; they are only 3 inches (7.5 cm) long but are a beautiful color and have a wonderful fragrance of ripe pineapple. We grow our plant with a *Clematis viticella* hybrid, making a beautiful display in early summer. One plant we know of withstood –12°F (–24°C) at Hendricks Park in Eugene, Oregon. *Cytisus battandieri* needs full sun and sharp drainage.

Origin: Morocco.
Hardiness: Zones 6–9.
Exposure: Sun.

Daphne

Where to start—or more likely, where to stop? We grow twenty-five or more different *Daphne* species or hybrids and can't imagine our garden without them. We have always grown *D. odora*, as did our relatives before us—for Roger, the smell of this species instantly brings back memories of his grandmother's garden in the early 1960s.

Depending on landscape size, climate zone, and soil drainage, numerous daphnes can be grown in the garden for months of beauty. These plants are native from western Europe all the way to eastern Asia. Most are evergreen, but several are deciduous, including *Daphne mezereum*, and they range in size from just 3 inches (7.5 cm) tall, *D. petraea*,

to 18 feet (5.5 m), *D. bholua*. The flowers can be white, pink, purple, or yellow in varying intensities. Many daphnes are fragrant, and the fragrance can carry through the whole garden.

Origin: Asia, Europe.
Hardiness: Zones 3–10.
Exposure: Sun to partial shade.

Daphne bholua. When we first saw this Himalayan species in the 1970s at Western Hills Nursery in Occidental, California, it was love at first sight (or smell). For us, *D. bholua* is just too tender for year-round survival outside. However, we always have several mature plants, 3–6 feet (0.9–1.8 m) tall, in containers to put near our homes. This daphne flowers from late fall well into late winter. The flowers are small clusters of pink-white. *Daphne bholua* is grown by more nurseries than it once was and should be much more available. Hardy in zones 7–8. Grow in partial shade.

Daphne genkwa (lilac daphne). This Chinese species has the most beautiful, soft lilac-purple wands of flowers in early spring. We originally received a plant from Reuben Hatch of Vancouver, Washington, in the late 1970s. We sold this species for a while, but it was extraordinarily difficult to propagate. Art Wright, then our propagator, rooted four hundred cuttings in 1981 or 1982, and we were thrilled. We saw the plants when they were in bloom, but to our frustration, two weeks later all but eight of them died. In the mid 1980s we found nine plants of a superior form in Portland. We tried cuttings of our

Daphne genkwa.

own and rooted 80 percent that grew on. *Daphne genkwa* is a deciduous plant of incredible refinement and beauty. Our plants have grown to 3–4 feet (0.9–1.2 m) tall with an open branching pattern. Lilac flowers clothe the stems in April. We have read about the Japanese using *D. genkwa* for flower arrangement but can't imagine cutting this lovely plant. Hardy in zones 5–8. Grow in sun to partial shade.

Daphne 'Lawrence Crocker'. This excellent dwarf daphne originally came from Law-rence Crocker, one of the founders of Sis-kiyou Rare Plant Nursery. In the 1960s and 1970s we would head to Lawrence's garden and nursery to buy alpines, then go get more plants from Boyd Kline, the other Siskiyou founder. We have seen 'Lawrence Crocker' as a mound of foliage 6 inches (15 cm) tall and 12 inches (30 cm) across. The dark ever-green leaves are narrow and make a perfect background for the sweetly scented, glowing pink flowers that cover the plant in April. Grow it in full sun for the fullest plant and most flowers. Hardy to zones 6–8.

Daphne 'Lawrence Crocker' at Buchholz and Buchholz Nursery in Gaston, Oregon.

Daphne mezereum. This species is native from northern Europe to Siberia and is hardy throughout the northern part of the United States and southern Canada. The healthiest specimens we've seen were in Richard Schultz's garden in Yakima, Washington. Our plants are 3–4 feet (0.9–1.2 m) tall and 2 feet (0.6 m) wide after ten years. The life span of the species is about ten to twelve years, but not to worry: it seeds prolifically, and birds scatter the seed around. Our friend in Yakima had plenty of plants, but since the seeds are heavy they didn't escape into the wild.

The leaves are 2–3 inches (5–7.5 cm) long and about ½ inch (1.25 cm) wide. Young, newly planted shrubs can become deciduous very early, in midsummer, so don't dig up a plant thinking it is dead. The deep purple-white flowers are borne in clusters along the preceding year's growth. Our plants start blooming in late fall and continue until early spring. The flowers are sweetly scented and cover the stems, making an attractive display. *Daphne mezereum* f. *alba* is a white-flowered form. Offspring are true to type: white-flowered plants produce white-flowered seed-

Daphne mezereum f. *alba.*

lings, and so forth. The fruit appears in early summer and by mid to late summer turns brilliant red (in purple-flowered plants) or amber (in white-flowered plants). Hardy in zones 3–8. Grow in sun.

Daphne odora. This Chinese native has been grown in the West since about 1770. It has one of the most intoxicating fragrances of any plant we grow, a combination of lemon, cinnamon, and other light scents. The evergreen foliage is dark green and glossy year-round. The plants can get to 4 feet (1.2 m) tall and 6 feet (1.8 m) across.

As for growing conditions, everything and nothing is correct. We have seen *Daphne odora* growing in full sun as well as full shade, in both lime soil and acid, with slow or fast drainage. It doesn't seem to make any sense, but this species sometimes succeeds in one person's garden but not in the garden next door to it. We recommend giving it filtered shade and well-drained acid soil, and then crossing your fingers. The enchanting fragrance of the purple and white late-winter flowers makes it worth the effort. At our nursery we give ourselves three attempts

Daphne odora 'Aureomarginata'.

at growing a plant; if we fail all three times, we give up. Hardy in zones 7–9.

Daphne odora 'Aureomarginata'. The typical variety grown in the United States and Canada. Golden yellow margins surround the dark green leaves. The flower petals are purple outside and snowy white inside. There are several English and Japanese variations with very wide yellow or cream leaf margins. Eric found an exceptional form, which we are testing. Grow in sun to partial shade.

Daphne odora.

***Daphne* ×*transatlantica* 'Jim's Pride'.** This superb deciduous shrub blooms in our region from early spring until hard frost. Our plants get to be 2–3 feet (0.6–0.9 m) tall and form an open growing mound. The gray-green leaves appear in early spring and make an excellent foil for the white flowers. Flowering usually starts slowly and builds to a massive bloom in late spring, after which there are sporadic blooms until late fall. The flowers aren't huge but are very fragrant and so prolific that we can't imagine our garden without this fine plant. Hardy in zones 5–9. Grow in sun.

***Daphne* ×*transatlantica* 'Summer Ice'.** A variegated form found by the late Bob Tichnor from Oregon State University's North Willamette Research and Extension Center in Aurora, Oregon. It is somewhat similar to *D.* ×*burkwoodii* 'Carol Mackie' but with broader leaves and a more rounded shape. The leaves are greenish gray with a broad margin of creamy white. This plant flowers all summer long. Grow in sun.

Desfontainia spinosa

This plant is fun to confuse even experienced gardeners with. It looks like a holly, with

The prolific white flowers of *Daphne* ×*transatlantica* 'Jim's Pride'.

hollylike prickles on its foliage, growing upright to maybe 8 feet (2.4 m) tall and 3 feet (0.9 m) wide. The difference, however, is in the flowers, which are 2 inches (5 cm) long, tubular, and dark orange with a yellow lip; they appear in early summer, continuing sporadically for a month. This unusual shrub was grown by Donald Stryker in Langlois, Oregon, in the 1960s but is still rare. It makes an interesting shrub in a large container. In the United States it is only hardy along the Oregon and California coasts.

Origin: Chile, Peru.
Hardiness: Zones 7–8.
Exposure: Partial shade.

Deutzia

Many gardeners believe deutzias are old-fashioned and hence not worth growing, but they can be stunning in bloom as practically no other plant group can. It is true they have a short bloom season of two to three weeks, but it is also true that many old roses, rhododendrons, and other plants are short bloomers and we still grow them. If you are willing to try some of the best deutzias, you will enjoy the prolific bloom they provide in late spring and early summer.

Origin: Asia.
Hardiness: Zones 4–9.
Exposure: Sun.

***Deutzia gracilis* 'Nikko'**. This Japanese cultivar is a very low growing deutzia for the front of the shrub border. We have seen plants 18 inches (45 cm) tall and 36 inches (91 cm) wide. The foliage is thick, full, and dark green all summer, in fall turning yellow with purple highlights. The flowers are like white stars in midspring and are so full that the foliage disappears behind them over most of the plant. An attractive ground cover around larger shrubs. The stems root down where they touch. Hardy in zones 4–9. Grow in sun.

***Deutzia* ×*hybrida* 'Magicien'**. We received this Victor Lemoine hybrid from Western Hills Nursery in the late 1970s. Our plant

Deutzia ×*hybrida* 'Magicien'.

is 10 feet (3 m) tall and 10 feet wide. Dark green leaves cover it all summer and make a great background for clematis. We thin out about one-third of our plant each winter, and this allows us to enjoy a massive bloom each spring. The flowers are deep pinkish purple in mid to late spring, and our plant weeps from the weight of the massive bloom. 'Magicien' is one of our most striking shrubs when in bloom. Very few plants produce as many flowers. It's always surprising how rarely we see deutzias like this in gardens, as they are very easy to grow, hardy, disease resistant, and gloriously beautiful. Hardy in zones 4–9. Grow in sun.

Deutzia scabra 'Candidissima'. We can't imagine many more flowers could cover this large shrub. Our plant is 10–12 feet (3–3.6 m) tall and 6 feet (1.8 m) across. We prune out old stems each spring to rejuvenate it. The dark green leaves are a nice backdrop for the racemes of double, white, late-spring flowers, which are so fluffy that they almost look like snow. *Clematis viticella* would be nice grown through this deutzia. Hardy in zones 4–9. Grow in sun.

Disanthus cercidifolius

We were introduced to this amazing foliage plant by our mentor Jane Platt. She was

The young green leaves of *Disanthus cercidifolius* turn purple by late summer.

generous in giving us cuttings, but despite several years of effort we were unable to propagate the plant ourselves. Reuben Hatch finally did the job, although we're still not sure how he did it—propagation is as much an art as it is a science.

This large shrub grows vase-shaped for many years, especially in lots of sun, but is eventually wider than tall, with tiers of foliage. The foliage is deep green and heart-shaped all summer, develops a purple blush somewhat like a plum by late summer, and gets progressively more colorful from late summer into fall. *Disanthus cercidifolius* has some of the most spectacular fall foliage of any plant we grow, becoming a kaleidoscope of orange, red, yellow, and purple. The flowers resemble witch hazel (*Hamamelis*) blooms but appear in early fall; they are tiny and do not have an appealing fragrance. The fruit appears the next summer and resembles small, fat hearts. Because of its great beauty, *D. cercidifolius* has been propagated by many growers and is widely available.

Origin: Japan, eastern China.
Hardiness: Zones 7–9.
Exposure: Partial shade.

As fall nears, *Disanthus cercidifolius* becomes a colorful blend of orange, red, yellow, and purple.

Drimys lanceolata (mountain pepper)

A Tasmanian native that reaches 8–10 feet (20–25 cm) over many years. The evergreen, peppery-scented foliage is very dark green year-round on this shrubby plant. The stems are a rich, deep purple. We hesitated to grow this species in our zone 7 garden, though it thrives in the Eugene-Springfield area. We may lose our plants at 0°F (–18°C), but *D. lanceolata* seems to grow fairly quickly. The white flowers are a bonus, as are the small black fruits. We have found a form with splashed variegation, 'Suzette', and hope to be able to propagate it as easily as the species. *Drimys lanceolata* makes an excellent potted plant for the patio. When tempera- tures drop below 15°F (–9°C), put it in an unheated garage.

Origin: Tasmania.
Hardiness: Zones 7–9.
Exposure: Sun to partial shade.

Edgeworthia

A small group of *Daphne* relatives from China. We first saw *E. chrysantha* at the North Willamette Research and Extension Center in Aurora, Oregon, in the late 1970s. The species we grow are multistemmed, deciduous shrubs up to 10 feet (3 m) tall. The foliage is medium green with a minor show of yellow in fall. Both *E. chrysantha* and *E. papyrifera* are hardy to zone 7 but

The unusual golden yellow flowers of *Edgeworthia chrysantha* have a slight fragrance.

need to be sited carefully, close to a building or evergreens.

Origin: China.

Hardiness: Zones 7–9.

Exposure: Sun to partial shade.

Edgeworthia chrysantha. The larger of the two species we grow, in terms of both plant and flower size. The stems are fairly large for the size of the plant. The new growth emerges in spring and branches into three stems during the growing season. Flowering begins in late winter and continues into spring. The golden yellow, slightly scented flowers are pendant, giving the plant an in-teresting look. Grow in sun to partial shade. Hardy in zones 7–9.

Edgeworthia papyrifera. The stems and foliage are much finer than those of *E. chrysantha*. The flowers are small and golden yellow, but sadly they have no fragrance. Pulmonarias look extremely handsome as a complementary planting under *E. papyrifera*. Hardy in zones 7–9. Grow in sun to partial shade.

Edgeworthia papyrifera 'Red Dragon'. The early-spring flowers of this selection aren't just red but a beautiful, orangey tomato soup color. 'Red Dragon' is smaller growing than the species. We have grown it for several

Edgeworthia papyrifera stems are finer than those of *E. chrysantha*.

Edgeworthia papyrifera 'Red Dragon'.

Left: *Elaeagnus ×ebbingei* 'Gilt Edge'.

years and find that it needs a very protected spot as it is more for zones 8–9. This fine plant is difficult to propagate and hasn't yet appeared in catalogs, but keep trying, as it is worth the search. Grow in sun to partial shade.

Elaeagnus ×ebbingei 'Gilt Edge'
The leaves of this cultivar are much broader than those of *E. pungens* 'Maculata'. They are also showier, with green centers and wide golden yellow margins. The overall effect is much more yellow than green.

Origin: Asia.
Hardiness: Zones 6–9.
Exposure: Sun to partial shade.

Elaeagnus pungens 'Maculata'

This is the most attractive *Elaeagnus* we grow. A native of Japan, it makes a large evergreen shrub up to 10 feet (3 m) tall and 8–10 feet (20–25 cm) across. The leaves are deep green at the margin and splashed with gold at the center. New growth is tan-bronze in early spring. 'Maculata' is a fast grower. It has thorns along the stems and can be used for a barrier. We use its long-lasting greens in flower arrangements.

Origin: Japan.
Hardiness: Zones 6–10.
Exposure: Sun to partial shade.

Eleutherococcus sieboldianus 'Variegatus'

An attractive plant for the shaded garden. This 3- to 4-foot (0.9 m to 1.2 m), upright, arching shrub has leaves with broad, creamy white margins. We have seen multiple cultivars listed as *E. sieboldianus* 'Variegatus', and most are more robust growers with narrow, cream to yellow margins. The form we grow was sent to us by J. C. Raulston in the early 1980s and is superior to any of the other forms of *Eleutherococcus* we have seen. It looks creamy white from a distance because of the wide margins. Our plants grow

Elaeagnus pungens 'Maculata'.

Eleutherococcus sieboldianus 'Variegatus' brightens the shady garden.

Opposite: *Embothrium coccineum*.

in heavy shade and make a perfect accompaniment for hostas and ferns.

Origin: Japan.

Hardiness: Zones 3–10.

Exposure: Shade.

Embothrium coccineum (Chilean fire bush)

Since this plant comes from southern Chile, we begin with a word of warning: it will not grow anywhere in the United States outside western Washington, Oregon, and northern California. People wanting to grow *E. coccineum* in the eastern part of the country will find that it dies as soon as it gets in the box and knows where it is going.

This is a striking plant. It can be a variety of sizes, from a 3- to 4-foot (0.9 m to 1.2 m) shrub to a 50-foot (15 m) tree. In the wild it is shrubby at high elevation and more tree-like close to the Pacific Coast.

We once had a tree from Lester Brandt in Federal Way, Washington. At the time we didn't know that embothriums are extraordinarily difficult to move, often dying immediately even when moved as small plants. We dug the plant, brought it home, and planted

it. After about a year it finally grew like crazy, and in the spring of 1972, at 40 feet (12 m) tall, its striking flowers bloomed. Our advice to you is to buy the smallest plant you can, and once you plant it, don't ever try to move it.

The foliage is narrow, perhaps ½ inch (1.25 cm) wide and 2–4 inches (5–10 cm) long. During summer it looks evergreen, but it does become deciduous in fall. The leaves slowly change from dark green to yellow but aren't showy.

The somewhat strange flowers are similar to those of *Grevillea*, another member of the protea family. They are composed of long tubes opening to reveal the stamens and curling back halfway down the bud. They appear in late spring and are somewhere between mandarin orange and red. Our plants are sometimes completely covered with flowers.

Although our plants initially bloomed in early summer, more recently they have come to bloom in late spring. When the bloom time changed, we found our *Embothrium coccineum* flowers coinciding with the medium pink flowers of *Rhododendron* 'Bow Bells'. The rhododendron has since been removed. Enough said.

Origin: Chile.
Hardiness: Zones 5–9.
Exposure: Sun to partial shade.

Enkianthus

This group of plants belongs to the Ericaceae and includes moderate-growing deciduous shrubs that are handsome year-round. In general, enkianthus have several upright stems with layered horizontal side branches.

Because of this tiered effect, the form of the plant is often as beautiful as the flower and foliage. We have seen thirty-year-old plants up to 15 feet (4.6 m) tall and 12–14 feet (3.6–4.3 m) wide, though most plants of *E. campanulatus* are 6–8 feet (1.8–2.4 m) tall. Enkianthus require the same conditions as rhododendrons, including plenty of moisture and well-drained soil. The narrow leaves are dark green all summer and make a superb show in October when they transition to attractive reds, oranges, and yellows. The small flowers appear in midspring and are bell- or urn-shaped. Some of the newer forms have rich red flowers, but most are a medium red-pink with white vertical shapes.

Origin: Japan.
Hardiness: Zones 5–9.
Exposure: Sun to partial shade.

***Enkianthus campanulatus* 'Red Bells'.** Many fine selections of *E. campanulatus* can be grown in the woodland garden. We grow several but don't see huge differences among them. Many have a limited production and so are only seen in collectors' gardens. 'Red Bells', however, seems to be the standard *Enkianthus* of the American nursery industry. Its foliage turns brilliant red every fall, and its small, bell-shaped, brilliant red flowers appear in midspring. Hardy in zones 4–9. Grow in sun to partial shade.

***Enkianthus campanulatus* var. *sikokianus*.** We like this variety for its larger leaves, which turn deep red-maroon in fall. The flowers are deep red and are larger than the species. Grow in partial shade.

Enkianthus campanulatus 'Variegatus'. We got this plant in the 1980s and so far it has grown to only 2–3 feet (0.6–0.9 m) tall. It has dark green leaves with a creamy yellow margin. Our plant has yet to flower, but the beautiful variegated leaves make it well worth growing. Grow in partial shade.

Enkianthus perulatus. This native of Japan is a superb dwarf shrub for the year-round garden, but it is also very slow growing, gaining

Small white urn-shaped flowers completely cover *Enkianthus perulatus* in late spring.

In fall the leaves of *Enkianthus perulatus* turn a brilliant orange-red.

3–6 inches (7.5–15 cm) per year. Our forty-year-old plant is about 4 feet (1.2 m) tall, and our plants from cuttings are 6–12 inches (15–30 cm) tall after three years. Most nurseries won't carry this plant because it grows too slowly to be profitable. Our rounded shrub is attractive during winter with its twiggy growth. In late spring, after it leafs out, the small white urns totally cover the plant for two to three weeks, and in fall the leaves turn brilliant orange-red for an extended season. All in all, this fine species is worth the effort it takes to find it. Hardy in zones 4–9. Grow in sun to partial shade.

***Enkianthus serrulatus*.** We received this large Chinese shrub from J. C. Raulston of the North Carolina State University Arboretum. J. C. liked to send care packages (our term) filled with cuttings and seedlings of new plants; he rarely sent anything that we already grew. We have grown *E. serrulatus* in semishade, and our plants are 5–6 feet (1.5–1.8 m) tall. The foliage is perhaps 3–4 inches (7.5–10 cm) long and deep green all summer, turning brilliant orange, red, and yellow in fall. The flowers are white and look like a giant version of those of *E. perulatus*. We haven't seen *E. serrulatus* listed in any other book or catalog, and it seems to remain infrequently grown. Hardy in zones 6–9.

Enkianthus serrulatus.

Exochorda ×macrantha 'The Bride' (pearl bush)

This cascading shrub is a real showstopper when in bloom in midspring. It can grow to 5–6 feet (1.5–1.8 m) tall with thin, arching branches and is beautiful planted at the top of a wall or pruned hard to a central trunk. The foliage is gray-green throughout summer. There is little fall color, but some of the annual vines or small summer-flowering clematis would add another season of interest if planted through 'The Bride'. Small white buds appear as the leaves expand in spring; these are borne like strings of pearls, hence the common name. The buds are attractive for an extended season before blooming, and the crenulated white flowers last for at least two weeks. We normally wouldn't recommend a plant with just one season of interest, but since this cultivar is so showy for such a long period, we feel it is garden worthy.

Origin: Garden origin.

Hardiness: Zones 4–8.

Exposure: Sun.

Fatsia japonica

This plant has almost everything a gardener could want. It can reach 15–18 feet (4.6–5.5 m) tall and is bushy as a youngster. As it matures it gets more open. If it gets too open, just cut the plant to 12 inches (30 cm) in spring and it will quickly regrow. *Fatsia ja-*

Exochorda ×macrantha 'The Bride'.

ponica has large, evergreen, maplelike leaves that are medium green. The flowers are small and creamy white on a large panicle up to 1 foot (0.3 m) long in late fall. Our plants froze to the ground at –12°F (–24°C) but by midsummer were back to 18 inches (45 cm) tall. This species can also make an attractive container plant for the house. It grows in semishade to deep, dark, north-facing shade.

We have seen plants that were thriving with heavy root competition.

Origin: Japan.

Hardiness: Zones 6–10.

Exposure: Partial shade.

Fatsia japonica 'Variegata'. We first saw and bought this neat plant at Western Hills Nursery in Occidental, California. The green maplelike leaves are broadly margined with creamy yellow, adding a bit of sparkle to this great evergreen. We strongly recommend this selection, particularly when compared with a selection called *F. japonica* 'Spider's Web', which looks more like spider mites to us, with its white-spotted green leaves. Grow in shade.

Fothergilla (dwarf alder)

Fothergilla major, *F. gardenii*, and *F. ×intermedia* are superb shrubs for gardens in all but the hottest, driest gardens. Growing anywhere from 18 inches (45 cm) to 14 feet (4.3 m) tall, these are suckering plants that slowly spread to form bushy, multistemmed shrubs. The white, paintbrush-like flowers are 2–3 inches (5–7.5 cm) long with narrow petals, and appear in early to midspring. The summer foliage is green, or in the case of *F. gardenii* 'Blue Mist' and *F. ×intermedia* 'Blue Shadow', powder blue. In midfall the foliage turns into a fireworks of orange, red, and yellow that lasts a fairly long time. In our experience *F. major* offers only yellow coloration when grown in shade and is more brightly colored when grown in sun.

Fatsia japonica 'Variegata'.

When we were first introduced to these fine plants by Jane Platt in the late 1970s, they were almost impossible to obtain or propagate. For years we imported them from Holland at great expense. Happily, since the tissue culture revolution in propagation, some of the fothergillas have become available from garden centers.

Origin: Southeastern United States.

Hardiness: Zones 5–9.

Exposure: Sun to partial shade.

***Fothergilla gardenii* 'Blue Mist'.** We have grown this cultivar for many years for its dusty blue foliage. It is a good plant for the woodland garden. The flowers are narrower and longer than most fothergillas. We have had spotty success growing it—some plants grow well, others do not. Our plants do well only in semishade; in sun the leaves become plain green.

***Fothergilla gardenii* 'Jane Platt'.** The smallest fothergilla we grow. We have plants that are 18 inches (45 cm) tall and 24 inches (61 cm) wide. This excellent selection is extremely adaptable. When we grow it in full sun next to pavement, it is very bushy and low growing. When we grow it in semishade, it is more cascading in form. The flowers are

Fothergilla gardenii 'Blue Mist'.

Fothergilla gardenii 'Jane Platt'.

typical of *F. gardenii*, white paintbrushes appearing in spring. Fall color lasts at least a month. The glorious combination of reds, oranges, and yellows can be a real showstopper at the edge of a border of larger shrubs. We are very happy that 'Jane Platt' has been such a good garden plant. We named it in the early 1980s after seeing Mrs. Platt's plants and taking cuttings. She was always so generous to us with cuttings, seeds, and information. Hardy in zones 5–9. Grow in sun to partial shade.

Fothergilla ×intermedia 'Blue Shadow'. Gary Handy of Boring, Oregon, heard our wishes for a blue fothergilla when he found this selection. A branch sport off of *F.* 'Mount Airy', it has larger oval leaves than *F. gardenii* 'Blue Mist'. The blue foliage is much more adapted to the sun than 'Blue Mist' and turns a beautiful dark red in fall. We still grow 'Blue Mist' in shady areas, but 'Blue Shadow' now occupies the sunnier spots of the garden.

Fothergilla major. When we initially started growing fothergillas, we grew *F. major*, *F. monticola*, and *F. gardenii*. *Fothergilla monticola* has since been lumped in with *F. major*.

Opposite top: The white bottlebrush-like flowers of *Fothergilla major*.

Opposite bottom: In fall *Fothergilla major* is a stunning blend of orange, red, and yellow.

This multistemmed, thicket-forming shrub is always attractive, with its gray bark and bushy habit, and can reach 8–15 feet (2.4–4.6 m) tall. The flowers are much larger and showier than those of *F. gardenii*. The foliage is deep forest green all summer and in fall turns into a kaleidoscope of red, orange, and yellow. Hardy in zones 5–9. Grow in sun to partial shade.

Fothergilla 'Mount Airy'. Michael Dirr found this selection at Mount Airy Arboretum in Cincinnati. After fifteen years our plants are irregular and upright in form, and 5–6 feet (1.5–1.8 m) tall. The foliage is dark green with a slight blush, in fall turning brilliant yellow, orange, and red. The flowers are the typical upright, white paintbrushes seen on most fothergillas. 'Mount Airy' is increasingly available in local garden centers and is being planted throughout the country. Grow in sun to partial shade.

Fremontodendron californicum (flannel bush)

This California native forms a large evergreen shrub. We have seen specimens in freeway plantings near Petaluma, north of San Francisco, that were 15 feet (4.6 m) tall and 15 feet wide. As we drove past them

Opposite: *Fothergilla* 'Mount Airy' compliments the fall color of *Stewartia pseudocamellia*.

Fremontodendron 'California Glory' flowers.

in May they were covered with golden yellow flowers.

We grew a flannel bush on a south-facing wall, and it survived 0°F (–18°C) with little damage. It was about 12 feet (3.6 m) tall and 4–5 feet (1.2–1.5 m) wide. We kept it narrow like an espalier against the wall. Unfortunately when we remodeled the house we had to remove this plant.

The leaves are very dark green year-round, deeply lobed, and covered with short hairs that can be irritating to the skin (be careful around your face and hands). The flowers are 2–3 inches (5–7.5 cm) across in late spring and a rich golden yellow. On our plants the flowers appear for at least a month and create quite a show.

We grow *Fremontodendron* 'California Glory', which is the most available form in nurseries along the Pacific Coast. We have also seen 'San Gabriel' and 'Pacific Sunset' in California, both of which are similar to 'California Glory'.

Fremontodendron californicum does well from California to western Oregon and Washington. We don't recommend trying it anywhere colder or more humid. It is easy to grow if given well-drained soil and full sun. It needs to be against a south wall but has proved much hardier than we expected it to be.

Origin: California.
Hardiness: Zones 7–10.
Exposure: Sun.

Gardenia jasminoides 'Kleim's Hardy'

This cultivar was discovered by Don Kleim of Henderson Experimental Gardens near Fresno, California. We first heard of it when Don brought one to us in the late 1980s. The small plant didn't look like much, but it grew steadily into a handsome evergreen shrub.

Our plants get to about 18 inches (45 cm) tall and 18 inches wide after several years. The deep green foliage is very glossy and covers the stems to make a bushy plant. We enjoy this shrub's long bloom season. The flowers occur sporadically through summer and only stop in fall at the first hard frost. The single, creamy white blossoms are deliciously scented even as they finally fade to tannish.

We feel lucky to be among the nurseries offering this excellent plant for the cooler (but not cold) garden. We know of plants that survived, in fact thrived, in 1991 when temperatures dipped to 0°F (–18°C). We grow our plants in afternoon shade to prolong the flowers and keep the glossy foliage from burning. This gardenia combines well with rhododendrons.

Origin: Garden origin in California.
Hardiness: Zones 7–10.
Exposure: Partial shade.

Garrya elliptica

This is one of our best native plants. We regularly see it on the southern Oregon coast and California coast. In Mendocino, California, we once saw plants all around U.S. Highway 1 that looked as though they were covered with icicles. These were in fact the buds and flowers.

Our plant is 15 feet (4.6 m) tall and 15 feet wide. It is an evergreen shrub with wavy, deep green, oval leaves that are somewhat rough like fine sandpaper. When the wind blows through *Garrya elliptica*, it makes a neat whirring sound.

We grow our plant in full sun with very little summer water. Our large overhead sprinklers form a V around it, so during summer it is essentially dry. We have also seen plants in semishade with heavier clay soil. These plants were more open and only 6–8 feet (1.8–2.4 m) tall.

The flower buds form in late summer to fall, and in mid to late winter the flowers form long, dangling catkins. The green individual flowers aren't too exciting, but the whole look of the catkins is very attractive

Garrya elliptica 'James Roof' catkins.

Garrya elliptica 'James Roof'.

in early spring. *Garrya elliptica* 'James Roof' is the most commonly cultivated plant of the genus.

Origin: California.
Hardiness: Zones 7–10.
Exposure: Sun to partial shade.

Gaultheria ×wisleyensis 'Wisley Pearl'

Discovered in 1929 at the Royal Horticultural Society's Wisley Garden, this moderate-growing shrub gets up to 2 feet (0.6 m) tall in our garden. Our plants are slowly spreading, suckering evergreen shrubs.

The leaves are small, dark green, and intermediate between those of the parents, *Gaultheria shallon* and *G. mucronata*. The small, white, urn-shaped flowers that appear in spring are a minor show. From late summer to fall 'Wisley Pearl' is covered with deep purple fruit. Our plants hold the fruit quite late in the fall.

We have seen plants that were full, bushy clumps 3–4 feet (0.9–1.2 m) across. Ours are more open and form thickets here and there. They have withstood –12°F (–24°C) with minimal damage. This selection needs moisture conditions similar to those required by rhododendrons.

Origin: Garden origin.
Hardiness: Zones 6–9.
Exposure: Partial shade.

Hamamelis (witch hazel)

Where do we start with one of our favorite plant groups? The witch hazel family, Hamamelidaceae, contains some of the most beautiful shrubs for our gardens, including *Hamamelis*, *Disanthus*, *Corylopsis*, and *Loropetalum* among others. Members of *Hamamelis* come from the southeastern United States, Mexico, Japan, and China, though for the most part we recommend and discuss the Japanese and Chinese species and hybrids.

We first saw *Hamamelis mollis* at Hendricks Park in Eugene, Oregon, in the late 1960s. It's interesting how learning about just one plant can lead to the discovery of a whole assortment of plants. After seeing *H. mollis*, we started to notice many more forms of *Hamamelis* in Portland and Seattle. Their winter blooms stirred a great interest in this great group of plants.

Plants of *Hamamelis mollis*, *H*. 'Brevipetala', *H*. ×*intermedia* 'Ruby Glow', and *H*. ×*intermedia* 'Jelena' that we acquired in Portland only made us want more, so we imported other forms from England and Holland. We now grow about forty species and hybrids, and we believe you can't ever have too many witch hazels.

These shrubs grow in an open vase shape and can reach 15–30 feet (4.6–9 m) tall and 10–15 feet (3–4.6 m) wide in thirty years. Our largest specimens were planted in the early 1970s and are 12–15 feet (3.6–4.6 m) tall and 14 feet (4.3 m) across.

Hamamelis foliage is oval and midgreen from spring to late summer. Fall coloration is yellow, orange, or red, or a mixture of these, depending on the species or hybrid. In general we find that varieties with darker red, orange, or purple flowers have darker orange-red leaves in fall, while yellow-flowered forms tend to have yellow-orange fall color.

The flowers are thin, twisted petals of yellow, orange, red, and purple. They bloom on bare branches in early to midwinter, a magical sight when practically no other tree or shrub shows color. We remember seeing *Hamamelis ×intermedia* 'Jelena' in Jane Platt's garden growing with *Prunus serrula* (paperbark cherry). It was a January day, 20°F (–7°C), and an arctic wind was blowing. The setting sun came through the shredding cherry bark and the witch hazel with stunning results.

The flowers of *Hamamelis* have varying amounts of fragrance. Some people can smell their sweet scent, while others cannot. In protected areas the scent can be lovely on a winter's day.

There is another exciting part of the *Hamamelis* experience: on a warm (50°F [10°C]) day in winter, the hard seed pods will explode, sending black seeds flying. If you are standing nearby you will hear the seeds whizzing by. This is especially fun indoors when seed pods in a flower arrangement fling seeds across the room.

Origin: Southeastern United States, Mexico, Japan, China.

Hardiness: Zones 5–8.

Exposure: Sun to partial shade.

***Hamamelis ×intermedia* 'Angelly'.** This superb witch hazel is relatively new to us. We first heard about it in the late 1990s and received our small, 6-inch (15 cm) plant from the Netherlands (the original seedling was raised in 1985 by J. H. M. van Heijningen in Breda). It is the last to bloom of any witch hazel we have, the flowers appearing when other selections are beyond their peak bloom. Brilliant yellow flowers cover this plant to the point that we can't see the stems.

'Angelly' is supposed to grow more slowly and stay smaller than most other witch hazels. For this reason it may be a good solution for those wanting smaller plants for a smaller garden. Grow in sun to partial shade.

***Hamamelis ×intermedia* 'Arnold Promise'.** Named in 1963 at the Arnold Arboretum in Boston, this is the standard witch hazel in

Hamamelis ×intermedia 'Arnold Promise'.

the United States. We see it in garden centers and nurseries more often than any other *Hamamelis*. Plants are upright and vase-shaped. We have seen them up to 15 feet (4.6 m) tall and 10 feet (3 m) wide. As with many witch hazels, this selection needs pruning to regenerate, so we cut out a few stems every two or three years to produce young, healthy wood. Bright, glowing yellow flowers appear in huge numbers, though they aren't as large as those of *H. ×intermedia* 'Sunburst'. The leaves are dark green and narrower than most *H. ×intermedia* types. Although the foliage of most yellow-flowering witch hazels is simply yellow in fall, 'Arnold Promise' adds orange and red to the mix. Grow in sun.

Hamamelis ×intermedia 'Diane'.

Hamamelis ×intermedia 'Diane'. A selection named in 1969 for Robert and Jelena de Belder's daughter. We first saw plants at Hollandia Gardens in Seattle, a great whole-

Hamamelis ×intermedia 'Diane' fall color.

sale source for new and unusual plants since the 1950s. We bought three specimens of 'Diane' in the late 1970s and saved two for our own garden. Those are now 12–14 feet (3.6–4.3 m) tall and 12–15 feet (3.6–4.6 m) wide. One plant is an upright vase shape, while the other is much more horizontal where it grows in shade. 'Diane' has the best fall color of all forms of *H. ×intermedia*, offering a blend of deep red, orange, and purple with yellow highlights. It is also the best red-flowering witch hazel we've seen. The flowers are deep red as the petals unfurl, but after two or three weeks they turn brick red and finally coppery orange. We find that red-flowering witch hazels need to be close

to the house or against a light background, since they disappear against a green background. Grow in sun to partial shade.

Hamamelis ×intermedia **'Jelena'**. Named for the great plantswoman Jelena de Belder of Belgium, 'Jelena' remains one of our best ornamentals after many years. We have one large plant that grows in almost all-day full sun. After thirty-five years it has reached 12 feet (3.6 m) tall and 15 feet (4.6 m) wide. The oval leaves are large, perhaps 3–4 inches (7.5–10 cm) long, and dark green, transitioning to a brilliant yellow-red in fall that lasts for an extended period. On our plant the flowers appear in late fall and last through

Hamamelis ×intermedia 'Jelena'.

midwinter. They are a lovely, vibrant coppery orange and cover the plant. Some people don't like this color, but in winter the orange is so warm it gives us the feeling that spring is coming. The flowers are sweetly scented at a time when we need their fragrance.

Hamamelis ×intermedia 'Sunburst'. Wow, what a flowering plant! This cultivar was named and introduced in 1967 by D. Veerman in Boskoop, Netherlands. It can have problems with its summer foliage, which can be contorted and not really attractive. Most years our plants look fine, other years not so much. However, the flowers are stunning enough to make this selection well worth growing. 'Sunburst' blooms are the largest and most prolific of any witch hazel we grow. They are bright golden yellow and positively glow during our cloudy, foggy winters in Oregon. When this cultivar is grown next to other witch hazels, it outshines all the other yellows we've seen. Some books describe it as holding onto its fall leaves, but almost all the leaves come off of our plants in winter. Grow it in sun to partial shade.

We suggest combining this witch hazel with one of the smaller *Clematis* selections, such as 'Étoile Rose' or other *C. texensis* hybrids. The clematis will be pruned in late fall, shortly before 'Sunburst' blooms in winter; and during summer the clematis will bloom with bright reddish pink bells that partially cover the witch hazel leaves.

Hamamelis vernalis 'Purpurea'. Although we don't normally recommend *H. vernalis* as a top-of-the-line shrub, 'Purpurea' is a superb ornamental. We first saw it at the Washington Park Arboretum in Seattle back in the 1970s. The plant structure is typical of the species, but the fall foliage is usually rich red-purple, occasionally yellow. The flowers are rich purple with a slightly pinkish flush. Our plant grows on the west side of our garden and is a wonderful sight in the afternoon sun. The flowers create a haze of color much like those of *Acer rubrum*. When visitors see our plant they always want their own, because the flowers are so different from any other witch hazel.

Hamamelis vernalis 'Sandra'. This Hillier Nurseries introduction was discovered by Peter Dummer in a block of *H. vernalis* seedlings in 1962. Mr. Dummer was scanning the green seedlings when he saw one plant that had purple new growth. The seedling was planted out and continued to show its purple new foliage in spring and summer. Another great attribute of this selection is its intense orange-scarlet fall coloration (*H. vernalis* is normally yellow in fall). The flowers are small and insignificant compared with the foliage.

In summer the leaves on our plants are purple until late in the season. When fall comes the new growth turns a shocking violet-purple with a scarlet background. Our plants have been very consistent in terms of leaf color. However, we have heard that in some areas, especially the southeastern United States, this coloration does not occur. We recommend it in our region, where it should be grown in sun to partial shade.

Hamamelis vernalis 'Sandra'.

Heptacodium miconioides (seven-sons flower)

We first received our plant in the mid 1980s and placed it in our well-drained soil in full sun. We were told to expect a plant up to 12–15 feet (3.6–4.6 m) tall, and ours exploded to 15 feet (4.6 m) tall and 6 feet (1.8 m) wide after eight years. Ultimately *H. miconioides* can reach 20 feet (6 m) in our climate, but we presume in colder or hotter climates it will get to 15 feet (4.6 m). It is very adaptable to cold and grows well in the upper Midwest and in the Southeast.

This upright-growing, shrubby tree has multiple trunks with attractive, creamy white to tan bark that exfoliates year-round. Its narrow, 6-inch-long (15 cm long) leaves are dark green during summer, turning rich yellow with pink highlights in fall. Small, white, pleasantly fragrant flowers appear in late summer in clusters. After the flowers fade, the seed forms and the sepals turn a rich pink, lasting until fall and adding another season of interest.

Origin: China.

Hardiness: Zones 4–9.

Exposure: Sun.

Hydrangea

This wonderful group of hardy plants is grown practically everywhere in the temperate garden world. Our gardens would be much poorer without their flowers and attractive foliage. Because hydrangeas are so different in terms of size, flower, and foliage, we will discuss their characteristics with each species or variety.

Origin: China, Japan, southeastern
    United States.
Hardiness: Zones 5–10.
Exposure: Sun to partial shade.

Hydrangea anomala subsp. **petiolaris** 'Mirranda'. Named by Guy and Jeanie Meacham of Rippingale Nursery in Boring, Oregon, for their daughter, this cultivar is similar to *H. anomala* subsp. *petiolaris* 'Platt's Dwarf' but probably slightly larger in all parts. The leaves are variegated, with an irregular patch of green surrounded by a wide, bright yellow margin from spring to midsummer. This hydrangea would be perfect in a dark, shady space. It can be grown on a wall or tree but not against a house, as the holdfasts on its stems would pull off the paint when removed. Hardy in zones 4–9.

Hydrangea anomala subsp. **petiolaris** 'Platt's Dwarf' (syn. *Schizophragma hydrangeoides* 'Platt's Dwarf'). We first saw this hydrangea in Jane Platt's garden in Portland, Oregon, in the 1970s growing over an 18-inch (45 cm) rock. The fine tracery of the rooted stems allowed the rock to be seen. The original plant has grown larger with age, but the stems are very thin and will creep up a wall or fence in some shade. The leaves are perhaps 1 inch (2.5 cm) long and ½ inch (1.25 cm) across. During summer they are deep green, and the edges are cut like someone took pinking

shears to them. In fall the foliage turns a rich butter yellow. We have rarely seen flowers on our plants, but when they appear they are small (3- to 4-inch [7.5 cm to 10 cm]) white clusters with many fertile flowers and a few sterile flowers. Hardy in zones 4–8. Grow in sun or shade.

Hydrangea arborescens 'Annabelle'. According to Linda Copeland and Allan Armitage in *Legends in the Garden*, the late great plantsman Joe McDaniel found 'Annabelle' in a garden in Urbana, Illinois, and traced it back to a garden in Anna, Illinois, where the plant was originally found in 1910. A mounding shrub, it reaches 5–6 feet (1.5–1.8 m) tall, with leaves that are light to medium green during summer. The flowers are large white pom-poms up to 8 inches (20 cm) across on mature plants. We grow 'Annabelle' as a perennial; after we cut it down each spring, it grows fast and blooms with huge 12-inch (30 cm) flowers by midsummer. The flowers appear on new growth, so cutting the plant down each year encourages extra large blooms. Hardy in zones 4–9. Grow in sun.

Hydrangea aspera. This group of supremely beautiful plants from western China can be upright shrubs when grown in light shade to almost full sun, or loose, broad-growing shrubs in full shade. The stems have slightly peeling bark in tans and browns. Most forms are upright and grow to 6–12 feet (1.8–3.6 m) tall, and all forms have hairy foliage. In summer the leaves are deep green. With too much sun the foliage burns very easily, so we suggest at least afternoon shade if not all-day shade. Fairly large lavender flowers appear in midsummer, with many fertile florets and a few sterile florets. All forms of *H. aspera* are worthy garden plants, but we have selected just a few. Hardy in zones 6–9.

***Hydrangea aspera* 'Macrophylla'.** One of the largest selections of any *Hydrangea* species, this shrub from western China grows to 15–18 feet (4.6–5.5 m) tall. Years ago we saw Reuben Hatch's plant at his Fruit Valley Nursery (now closed); it was in full sun and probably 18–20 feet (5.5–6 m) tall and 6–8 feet (1.8–2.4 m) across. The dark green leaves of 'Macrophylla' are fascinating because they look just green at first but have purple and pink on the hairs. The leaves can be 10 inches (25 cm) long and 4 inches (10 cm) wide. The flowers are up to 10 inches (25 cm) across, with lots of fertile florets and a few lavender sterile florets. Hardy in zones 6–8. Grow in partial shade.

***Hydrangea aspera* subsp. *sargentiana*.** Another very rare plant in the *H. aspera* group. Ours has large, stout leaves that are almost as wide as they are long. The stems are hairy like the foliage. The flowers are similar to *H. aspera* 'Macrophylla' but very light grayish lavender. It took us years to find the true *H. aspera* subsp. *sargentiana*, as most plants of *H. aspera* 'Macrophylla' are mislabeled as this subspecies. The flower color and foliage are very different in these two plants. Hardy in zones 6–8. Grow in partial shade.

Hydrangea aspera subsp. *sargentiana*.

Hydrangea macrophylla 'Pia'. This is the smallest hydrangea we grow. Our biggest plant is 18–24 inches (45–61 cm) tall after many years. This slow-growing selection seems to be very hardy, easy to grow, and quick to bloom. The leaves are dark green all summer and make a great background for the 3-inch (7.5 cm) mophead flowers, which are pink-purple (with the exact color depending on the soil). 'Pia' makes an excellent plant for even the smallest container or garden. Hardy in zones 5–10. Grow in sun to partial shade.

Hydrangea paniculata 'White Moth'. We have seen *H. paniculata* 'Grandiflora', the so-called peegee hydrangea, in gardens throughout the country; it is very hardy even in some of the coldest areas, and in time becomes a small tree with long, white summer flowers. 'White Moth' is a much improved cultivar of the same species. Our twenty-year-old plant is 12 feet (3.6 m) tall and 4–5 feet (1.2–1.5 m) across. It isn't a fabulous-looking specimen after blooming, and we wouldn't normally recommend such a plant for just one

Hydrangea 'Preziosa' growing with *Berberis thunbergii* 'Royal Cloak' at the Bellevue Botanical Garden in Bellevue, Washington.

season. However, 'White Moth' has such enormous, striking flowers that we strongly recommend it over other *H. paniculata* cultivars. The flowers can be over 12 inches (30 cm) across when they bloom in early to midsummer. 'White Moth' is also hardy and fast growing, with deep green leaves. What more can we ask of a garden plant? Hardy in zones 4–9. Grow in sun.

Hydrangea 'Preziosa'. A 4-foot (1.2 m) upright grower with deep green leaves tinted purple from spring through summer. By fall the foliage turns a beautiful, rich purple-red. The mophead flowers are small like those of *H. macrophylla* 'Pia', but showier, varying from light pink to deeper pink, purple to blue. The color change can be all on one plant, and though this sounds garish, it is actually very pretty. Grow in partial shade.

Hydrangea quercifolia (oak leaf hydrangea). An excellent garden plant for much of the country, this American native is an irregular, upright grower to 8–10 feet (20–25 cm) tall, especially when given some shade. We have seen it growing in both heavy shade and full sun in nursery rows. The leaves resemble those of an oak, with deep indentations along the margins. They are deep green all summer and by mid to late fall turn rich orange-red and purple. In protected gardens or warm climates the leaves sometimes hold their color until midwinter. The white paniculate flowers have many sterile florets and are quite showy when they show up in midsummer.

Hydrangea quercifolia 'Brihon' (Little Honey). We first saw this form in 2004. Although it hasn't been tested, we list it here because it is so exciting to have a golden-leaved hydrangea. It has all the features of *H. quercifolia* in terms of stem, flower, foliage, and shape, but the leaves are a gorgeous golden yellow. It will be interesting to see how well this plant does in gardens. Hardy in zones 4–9. Grow in partial shade.

Hydrangea quercifolia Snow Queen. This form was discovered and named by Princeton Nurseries in Princeton, New Jersey, a large wholesale nursery. It seems to have become the standard *H. quercifolia* of the nursery industry throughout the country. It is a hardy (to −22°F [−30°C], according to Michael Dirr), fast grower with white, upright, 8- to 10-inch (20 cm to 25 cm) flowers. The flowers are covered with sterile florets that create a beautiful display without weighing down the panicle and making it droop. They turn tan by fall, continuing the display. Thanks to tissue culture, *H. quercifolia* Snow Queen and many other plants, from kalmias to rhododendrons, are much more available than they once were. Hardy in zones 5–9. Grow in sun to partial shade.

Hydrangea serrata 'Blue Billow'. We heard about this cultivar from several gardeners and finally bought a plant from Heronswood Nursery in Kingston, Washington. Our impressions are that it's a first-rate shrub. Our plants grow in light shade and are 18 inches (45 cm) tall and 36 inches (91 cm) across. The spectacular foliage is as showy as any *H.*

quercifolia. It is jagged at the edge and dark green all summer, turning deep red-purple by late summer and early fall. The lacecap flowers are midblue from early to midsummer and form a beautiful blue frosting during summer. In the past we tried to prune our plants like we do for *H. macrophylla*, but there were too many stems, so it took too long and didn't work. We found that we could just let the plants grow on their own without pruning. Every five or six years we cut our plants to the ground in early spring. We don't get flowers the first year, but the following five or six years bring heavy blooms and beautiful foliage. Hardy in zones 6–10.

The jagged leaves of *Hydrangea serrata* 'Blue Billow' turn deep red-purple in fall.

Hydrangea serrata 'Blue Billow' in flower.

Ilex (holly)

This genus includes many evergreen and a few deciduous shrubs to small trees for almost any landscape. Most people think of hollies for their beautiful foliage and fruit for the Christmas season. There are, however, many hollies that can be grown for their unusual form and foliage.

Origin: Japan.
Hardiness: Zones 5–9.
Exposure: Sun.

Ilex crenata. Discovered in Japan in the late 1700s, this important species can form an upright shrub 18–20 feet (5.5–6 m) tall or a mounding, small or dwarf shrub. All forms of *I. crenata* have small evergreen leaves. The plants are hardy and very easy to grow in full sun to semishade. We have chosen two cultivars for their unusual structure.

Ilex crenata 'Dwarf Pagoda'. This is a most unlikely holly for its deep green leaves, each of which is nearly plastered against the next leaf below it. We regularly fool gardeners by asking them to identify this cultivar, which they usually guess is a hebe or some other strange plant. When we talked about this plant years ago with James Cross of Environmentals Nursery in New York, he told us that a nursery would take cuttings from 'Dwarf Pagoda', throw the longest ones away, and keep the tiniest ones in order to grow the smallest plant possible. If long cuttings are

Ilex crenata 'Dwarf Pagoda'.

taken and rooted, within four or five generations this holly will get to 15 feet (4.6 m) tall rather than remaining 3–5 feet (0.9–1.5 m). Most nurseries don't carry 'Dwarf Pagoda' because they can't make a profit selling two-year-old plants. We like it so much for its handsome compact growth and beautiful dark green foliage that we continue to grow it even though it isn't really profitable for us. It makes a neat garden shrub or a wonderful container plant for the patio.

Ilex crenata 'Sky Pencil'. This is one of the easiest plants to propagate and grow into a narrow sentinel. We have grown it for about twenty-five years and now have 8- to 9-foot (2.4 m to 2.7 m) plants that are 18 inches (45 cm) wide. These plants are a strong focal point in our garden, planted in a trio at the beginning of a path. We have also used three plants spaced out to control and highlight the view east toward the Cascades. 'Sky Pencil' makes a nice, fairly quick-growing hedge with fine foliage and upright growth. People are often put off by conifer hedges, and this holly offers an attractive alternative. 'Sky Pencil' also makes a good container plant. We have suggested using it against a south-facing wall, and people can't believe how well it grows where hardly any other plant is happy. Hardy in zones 5–9. Grow in sun.

Ilex serrata and ***I. verticillata*** (winterberry holly). These large, deciduous American natives look so beautiful in garden books. Our

Ilex crenata 'Sky Pencil'.

problem is that when the red, yellow, or orange fruits change color in fall, birds come from throughout the area to immediately pick every plant clean. We recommend the winterberry hollies for the Northeast and Midwest, where birds don't seem to eat all the fruit. We wish these hollies could do well in our garden, but we haven't had any luck when it comes to birds, which seem to need the fruit more than we do. Please also see Michael Dirr's *Manual of Woody Landscape Plants.*

Illicium anisatum

This fine Japanese native can reach 10 feet (3 m) tall in forty years. It has been grown in Portland, Oregon, since the 1950s, so must be able to withstand temperatures as low as −10°F (−23°C), and is hardy in zones 7–9. *Illicium anisatum* makes a full, bushy, attractive plant with 3-inch, glossy, medium green leaves that are very fragrant when crushed in your hand. The flowers are little (1 inch [2.5 cm] long), multipetalled, creamy white stars, and on our plants last for at least a month from early to midspring. We grow *I. anisatum* in filtered shade in the heat of the day. Even though this adaptable evergreen shrub has been in the United States a long time, it is rarely seen. We think it should be grown much more frequently.

Origin: Japan.

Hardiness: Zones 6–9.

Exposure: Partial shade.

Illicium anisatum.

Illicium floridanum

This American native grows to 8 feet (2.4 m) tall over time. It will grow in full sun all day in our climate with no burning, but is happier with some afternoon shade. The leaves are 3–6 inches (7.5–15 cm) long and deep matte green throughout the year. This is an excellent substitute for photinia, as it grows in a range of conditions. It can be sheared to make it more compact. The flowers are deep red-purple stars more than double the size of those of *I. anisatum*. They appear in late spring and bloom sporadically through midsummer.

Several selections are available. *Illicium floridanum* 'Halley's Comet', found by the late nurseryman John Allen Smith of Mobile, Alabama, produces large amounts of flowers that are bigger than those of the species. *Illicium floridanum* f. *album* has ivory white flowers that are the same size as those of *I. floridanum*, but it is much hardier than *I. anisatum*.

We suspect illiciums will be the plants of the future, as more selections are made in the wild and in gardens. They are hardy, disease resistant, and easy to grow. Their evergreen leaves are attractive all year, and in spring to early summer the flowers are very different from other evergreens.

Origin: Southern United States.
Hardiness: Zones 6–9.
Exposure: Sun to partial shade.

Itea ilicifolia (holly-leaf itea)

This species is an open grower to 8–10 feet (20–25 cm) tall and wide. Its glossy, dark green leaves have wavy margins edged with soft spines. These spines aren't like those on a barberry but are bendable and give the leaf a beautiful edge. Early in summer the long, narrow racemes appear. The greenish yellow flowers can be up to 14 inches (36 cm) long and are showy for about a month. The main reason *I. ilicifolia* isn't grown more often is its semihardy nature. In the Seattle area, Oregon, coastal California, and the Gulf Coast, it is glorious. We have grown it for years in a container, and its flowers drip to the ground.

Origin: China.
Hardiness: Zones 8–10.
Exposure: Partial shade.

Itea virginica (Virginia sweetspire)

This suckering shrub can grow as tall as 6 feet (1.8 m), though is usually shorter, and is generally wider than tall. Its narrow, spineless foliage is deep green all summer and can transition to attractive purple, reds, and yellows before falling. Our plants don't generally lose all their leaves until the new foliage emerges. *Itea virginica* has white racemes in early summer that are arching and lightly fragrant. Since the 1980s, several handsome selections have been named, further expanding the range of this fine species.

Origin: Eastern United States.
Hardiness: Zones 5–9.
Exposure: Sun to partial shade.

Itea virginica 'Henry's Garnet'. This bushy plant was discovered in the 1980s at Swarthmore College in the Philadelphia area. It grows to 3 feet (0.9 m) tall and 3–4 feet (0.9–1.2 m) wide with rich purple foliage in fall.

Opposite: *Itea virginica* 'Henry's Garnet' in fall.

Kalmia latifolia (mountain laurel)

The evergreen foliage of this species is usually dark green and glossy like a rhododendron and is sometimes rough in texture. Beyond the typical light pink flowers that open white, kalmias can have red buds, split petals, and purple spots creating bands around the flower. The trusses of flowers bloom in late spring, with individual blossoms resembling small parachutes, the stamens stuck inside little pockets in the petals. When a bee visits, the pollen is hurled out at it, ensuring that the pollen is carried to the next flower. This can be something fun for children to see.

A thank you must go to Dick Jaynes of Connecticut's Broken Arrow Nursery, father of the modern mountain laurel. Over the years Jaynes has collected and bred an enormous range of plants and flowers. The tissue culture revolution has also played a role in the huge upswing of these plants. Before tissue culture, kalmias were rare and difficult to propagate.

Origin: Eastern United States.
Hardiness: Zones 5–9.
Exposure: Partial shade.

Kalmia latifolia 'Elf'. One of the smallest growers, this upright plant can eventually

get to 2–3 feet (0.6–0.9 m) tall. The flower buds are light pink, opening to pure white. A good plant for even the smallest garden. Provide afternoon shade.

Kalmia latifolia 'Ostbo Red'. An oldie but goody, this Pacific Northwest selection has been around our gardens for many years. It was the first red-budded form to become available. The deep red buds open to flowers that are light pink to white. Grow in partial shade.

Kalmia latifolia 'Pristine'. Found in South Carolina by the folks at Woodlanders Nursery, Aiken. Though we haven't seen this plant, we list it because of its heat tolerance.

It is 4 feet (1.2 m) tall and wide and has pure white flowers. It should grow well throughout the Southeast as well as further north, performing best in partial shade.

Kalmia latifolia 'Sarah'. Our favorite of all the mountain laurels we've grown. The foliage is deep green and glossy. The flowers are red and open to deep pink in mid to late spring. This cultivar was named by Dick Jaynes and is one of his greatest introductions. Grow in partial shade.

Kerria japonica

As the name implies, this species is native to Japan. It is a deciduous shrub that can get up to 8 feet (2.4 m) tall. The stems are bright

Kalmia latifolia 'Sarah'.

spring green and make a nice statement in winter. The leaves are narrow and about 2 inches (5 cm) long with jagged edges; they are dark green and don't offer much fall color. The flowers are a bright golden yellow and usually 2 inches (5 cm) across in mid-spring. 'Pleniflora' is the most typically seen *K. japonica*; to us, however, its double flowers are garish.

Origin: Japan.
Hardiness: Zones 5–9.
Exposure: Sun to partial shade.

Kerria japonica 'Albiflora'. This plant originally came to us in one of J. C. Raulston's care packages. It is a 3- to 4-foot (0.9 m to 1.2 m) shrub with a light texture and form. The single flowers, which are wavy and white in midspring, are so simple and beautiful that this shade lover can really add to the spring garden. Grow in sun to partial shade.

Kerria japonica 'Golden Guinea'. This cultivar originated in Japan and China and came to us from Pieter Zwijnenburg of Boskoop, Netherlands. The foliage and form are typical of the species, but the large, bright golden yellow flowers are single and 2 inches (5 cm) across. The flowers are all the more brilliant with the deep green leaves as a backdrop. Hardy in zones 4–9. Grow in sun to partial shade.

Kolkwitzia amabilis (beauty bush)

E. H. Wilson found this plant in China in 1901. He considered it one of his finest introductions—quite a statement, considering he introduced more than four hundred plants.

This 8- to 10-foot (2.4 m to 3 m) shrub is often sheared. It should be allowed to grow as an open shrub to show off its flowers to best effect. The leaves are 1½ inches (4 cm) long and ½ inch (1.25 cm) wide. The matte green foliage isn't exciting in either summer or fall, but soft light pink flowers cover the plant during early summer, making up for the dull foliage.

Origin: Western China.
Hardiness: Zones 4–8.
Exposure: Sun.

Kolkwitzia amabilis Dream Catcher ('Maradco'). This fairly new shrub looks to us like a real winner. The plant size and flower color are similar to *K. amabilis* 'Pink Cloud', but the bronze-pink new foliage turns a pretty golden color in summer. We expect Dream Catcher to become a standard landscape plant. Grow in sun.

Kolkwitzia amabilis 'Pink Cloud'. Named in 1946 at the Royal Horticultural Society's Wisley Garden, England, this rich-pink–flowering shrub is a great improvement over the species. In fact we didn't think *K. amabilis* was worth growing until we saw 'Pink Cloud'. In early summer it is covered with thousands of pink flowers, and planting an annual vine through it might give another season of interest later in the year. Grow in sun.

Lavatera ×*clementii* 'Barnsley'

This lavatera grows to 6 feet (1.8 m) or so in full sun to light shade. The medium green leaves hold on until late fall; they are deciduous or at least semievergreen in warmer climes. The flowers look like hollyhocks in early to midsummer, with light pink petals and a deep pink center, covering the plant for weeks and making an excellent show in the perennial border or with other shrubs. 'Barnsley' can revert to the look of *L.* ×*clementii*, so it's best to prune out any stems that have plain pink flowers.

Origin: Garden origin in Europe.
Hardiness: Zones 7–10.
Exposure: Sun.

Lavatera thuringiaca

Lavateras are not appreciated enough for their quick growth and heavy flowering over a long season. We realize these plants are short lived (three to four years), but don't many gardens contain annuals or biennials? Lavateras such as *L. thuringiaca* give a big bang for the gardener's buck. If nothing else, mix slower-growing and longer-lived plants and use several lavateras in between. After a few years, pull out the lavatera (an easy task, since they don't have large roots). An instant plant, *L. thuringiaca* can grow from a 1-gallon plant to a glorious 6-foot (1.8 m) shrub in one year.

Origin: Europe.
Hardiness: Zones 5–10.
Exposure: Sun.

Lavatera thuringiaca 'Ice Cool'. We shouldn't dismiss a plant just because it is common and easy to grow. This pure-white–flowered mallow is a real showstopper. The flowers actually sparkle in late spring and early summer.

Another useful, beautiful plant for the summer garden. Grow in sun.

Leiophyllum buxifolium

A small-growing shrub from the Pine Barrens of southeastern New Jersey. It is very slow growing but worth the wait. Our plants are 12–18 inches (30–45 cm) tall after many years in the garden. *Leiophyllum buxifolium* forms an upright mound that looks vaguely like a hebe, though it is dramatically hardier. The evergreen leaves are 1/4 inch (0.6 cm) long and bronze in spring, turning dark, glossy green in summer. The flowers appear in small (1-inch [2.5 cm]) white trusses in midspring and combine beautifully with the bronze new foliage. We have not seen any selections of *L. buxifolium*—perhaps this species has very little variation? We grow it with our rhododendrons in well-drained, humus-amended soil. We don't recommend *L. buxifolium* for hot or dry climates, as it will suffer from burn or root rot.

Origin: Eastern United States.
Hardiness: Zones 5–9.
Exposure: Partial shade.

Lespedeza thunbergii (bush clover)

This species can be grown as a shrub or cut back each spring to make a fast-growing perennial. We have grown several cultivars without success. *Lespedeza thunbergii* prefers full hot sun. Our cool summers, with nighttime temperatures around 50°F (10°C), do not allow it enough time to bloom.

Origin: China, Japan.
Hardiness: Zones 5–9.
Exposure: Sun.

Lespedeza thunbergii 'Gibraltar'. We highly recommend this cultivar, which has grown for many years in our garden and bloomed spectacularly each late summer. Our plants get 8 feet (2.4 m) across, and when cut back in spring still grow to 6–8 feet (1.8–2.4 m) tall. We don't have any walls over which to cascade plants, but that would be a great way to use 'Gibraltar'. The pealike flowers are rich purple in mid to late summer and cover our plants for more than a month. These flowers are perfect combined with *Miscanthus* (maiden grass) flower heads, *Patrinia scabiosifolia*, and other late-summer plants. *Lespedeza thunbergii* 'Gibraltar' is a hardy, easy, fast-growing plant that takes full hot sun and thrives on adversity. Even though it needs to be watered in summer, it makes an excellent show for difficult areas. Hardy in zones 5–9.

Leucothoe

A small genus of beautiful evergreen shrubs, including our native *L. fontanesiana* from the Appalachians. These woodland plants usually have an arching habit, attaining a height of

The cascading purple flowers of *Lespedeza thunbergii* 'Gibraltar' combine beautifully with the yellow flowers of *Solidago rugosa* 'Fireworks'.

1–8 feet (0.3–2.4 m) depending on the species. The clusters of white flowers that appear in late spring are arching, terminal sprays except in *L. davisiae*, which has upright racemes. Most species of *Leucothoe* want well-drained but moist soil year-round.

Origin: Japan, China, United States.
Hardiness: Zones 4–10.
Exposure: Partial shade.

Leucothoe davisiae (Sierra laurel). As its common name implies, this Californian species is native to the Sierra Nevada. We first saw it complementing a group of shaded steps in

the garden of Jane Platt, who had used it as an informal ground cover. This species grows to 12–18 inches (30–45 cm) tall, with deeply veined, medium glossy green, evergreen foliage. The flowers hold on for a long time when the plant is grown as it was in Mrs. Platt's garden, as a large-scale ground cover in an informal area under small trees and large shrubs. Hardy in zone 8. Grow in partial shade.

Leucothoe keiskei. This Japanese native is the smallest *Leucothoe* species: our biggest plant is 1 foot (0.3 m) tall and 1 foot wide. We had a hard time finding it originally, and our first plant was only 2 inches (5 cm) tall. We later received a more robust form that is a much better garden performer. The stems arch like those of *L. fontanesiana* but even more so. The glossy evergreen foliage is reddish purple when new, becomes deep green later in summer, and in fall turns deep purple. Fairly large racemes of white, bell-like flowers appear in late spring. *Leucothoe keiskei* needs good drainage and a compost-based soil that is moist through the summer months. We don't recommend growing this fine plant in the Southeast or in dry regions, as it wants cool soil and shade. In the areas where it is hardy, zones 6–9, *L. keiskei* is a real charmer for the shady border or rock garden. Grow in partial shade.

Lindera obtusiloba (spice bush)
There are many Asian and American *Lindera* species, but we have chosen to focus on

Lindera obtusiloba.

our favorite, a species from China. This large shrub usually has several upright trunks with horizontal side branches. Our original plant grew to 12 feet (3.6 m) tall after fifteen years in semishade. However, since we mistakenly thought *L. obtusiloba* was a much smaller shrub, we replaced that plant with a new one that will have much more room. The foliage is medium green and can be heart-shaped, oval, or mitten-shaped—it's fun to show children all the different leaf shapes. In fall the leaves turn a wonderful golden yellow. In late winter to early spring hundreds of golden yellow flowers appear on the bare branches, looking like a hazy mist. The flowers vaguely resemble those of *Cornus mas*.

Origin: China, Japan, Korea.
Hardiness: Zones 6–9.
Exposure: Sun to partial shade.

Lomatia myricoides

This member of the protea family comes to us from southeastern Australia. The plant we grow is upright, 8 feet (2.4 m) tall, and 4–5 feet (1.2–1.5 m) wide after fifteen years against a south-facing wall. In a mixed border it makes an attractive foliage plant year-round. The leaves are narrow, 1/2 inch (1.25 cm) wide and 4 inches (10 cm) long, gray-green, and jagged along the margin. Small, ivory white flowers appear in early summer, and although they aren't showy, their vanilla fragrance is wonderful. Our plant came from the Washington Park Arboretum in Seattle, where *L. myricoides* has been grown since at least the 1960s. The main problem with this species is that it can't take nitrogen. We forgot this fact once and fertilized our young

plants. Within a week they were all black and dead. Rather than fertilizing, we just grow our plants in amended sandy loam, and they thrive. They have withstood 0°F (–18°C).

Origin: Southeastern Australia.
Hardiness: Zones 6–8.
Exposure: Partial shade.

Lonicera (honeysuckle)

Honeysuckles are extremely well known in gardens throughout temperate regions and need little introduction. These are typically scrambling vines with dark green summer leaves, but there are also evergreen and deciduous shrubby forms. The long, tube-shaped flowers bloom in early summer and are very fragrant on many varieties. Other honeysuckles have smaller flowers that appear from late spring to early summer. We describe two very different species that have grown well for us.

Origin: China.
Hardiness: Zones 4–8.
Exposure: Sun.

Lonicera fragrantissima. This excellent winter-flowering shrub from China can reach 10–12 feet (3–3.6 m) tall in time. We prune our plant regularly to keep new stems growing and maintain a height of 4–6 feet (1.2–1.8 m). When young, our nursery plants look like vines, and sometimes customers insist we have mislabeled them. But as the plants mature, they form a woody frame. Their deep green, oval leaves turn golden yellow in fall. The flowers are typical of honeysuckles in terms of shape but are pure white during winter. They aren't large, perhaps 1/2 inch

Lonicera fragrantissima.

(1.25 cm) wide, but are extraordinarily fragrant at a time when we don't expect to find sweet-smelling flowers. *Lonicera fragrantissima* isn't too pretty out of bloom during the rest of the year, so we suggest combining it with *Clematis alpina*, which flowers in early spring. Grow in sun.

Lonicera nitida 'Baggesen's Gold'. This doesn't look anything like a honeysuckle. We have seen 6- to 8-foot (1.8 m to 2.4 m) shrubs that were left to grow naturally. We have also seen plants grown as hedging in France that were less than 1 foot (0.3 m) tall. The tiny, glossy leaves are golden yellow and thick year-round, so the plant is bushy and full. This easy grower is a great garden plant with only one minor fault: the tiny flowers are not visible. Grow in sun to partial shade.

Loropetalum chinense (Chinese fringe flower)

When we first heard of this plant in the early 1980s, we couldn't find it outside of Europe. A revolution came to the world of *Loropetalum* later that decade, and purple-leaved forms started to show up in public gardens. They grow to be about the same size as the green-leaved forms.

Loropetalum chinense is a broad, horizontal to slightly weeping plant. It grows to 4–5 feet (1.2–1.5 m) tall in our area, but we were shown a 20-foot (6 m) tree in the warmer climate of Aiken, South Carolina, by the folks at Woodlanders Nursery. The dark green or purple leaves are oval and 1 inch (2.5 cm) long, though some of the purple varieties can have longer, narrower leaves. This witch hazel (*Hamamelis*) relative has the typical narrow, strap-shaped flowers, which are pure white through deep pink in late spring.

We have grown the form from Hillier Nurseries for many years, and our plants only get to 2 feet (0.6 m) tall and 3–4 feet (0.9–1.2 m) wide. The leaves are deep green through the year. Attractive, narrow, white, strap-shaped flowers appear in late spring.

In our garden, loropetalums are hit by frosts most winters but regrow quickly in spring. We usually plant ours in containers, where they are lovely year-round.

Origin: China.

Hardiness: Zones 7–10.

Exposure: Sun to partial shade.

Loropetalum chinense 'Sizzling Pink'. Found and named by Mark Krautmann of Heritage Seedlings in Salem, Oregon. We include this purple-leaved form because it is available in our area, but different selections will be available in other parts of the country. 'Sizzling Pink' is wider than high and has rich purple new growth that fades a bit during summer. Grow in sun to partial shade.

Magnolia

Where to start with our favorite group of plants? These are normally medium to large trees, and many are subtropical or tropical and too tender and large to write about in this book. Most have medium to dark green, oblong, deciduous leaves. Sometimes the leaves are incredibly huge, as with *M. macrophylla*. Magnolias bloom from early spring until late summer, and the flowers are among the most sensational of any hardy tree. The flowers can be up to 15 inches (38 cm) across, although most are 4–10 inches (10–25 cm) across, and are white, yellow, pink, purple, or a mix of these colors. Rather than having distinct petals, the blossoms have tepals, which are adapted sepals. Magnolias need good drainage but can grow in a wide range of soils. Many are hardy to zone 5, and hybridizers continue to push their hardiness.

We have chosen to describe several varieties that will stay under 20 feet (6 m) tall with minor pruning. These may seem a bit large, but we find it impossible to resist such voluptuous flowers. On this note, we have a recommendation for the great magnolia hybridizers of the United States, New Zealand, and elsewhere: please breed magnolias that are small in stature. We consistently have customers wanting 10- to 15-foot (3 m to 4.6 m) magnolias for their urban or suburban gardens. Now, off our soap box.

Origin: China, Japan, southeastern
United States.
Hardiness: Zones 4–10.
Exposure: Sun to partial shade.

Magnolia Kosar/de Vos hybrids. These crosses between *M. liliiflora* and *M. stellata*, as well as some of their cultivars, result from breeding work conducted in the 1950s by William Kosar and Francis de Vos at the U.S. National Arboretum. When we first grew these magnolias we didn't like them as much as we do now. They become handsome, multi-trunked, large shrubs as they mature. The form is probably more like *M. stellata*. The foliage is very similar to *M. liliiflora* (in fact we can't see much difference). The flowers look like those of *M. liliiflora*, but the plant is heavier flowering like *M. stellata*. The flower color ranges from lavender-purple to deep, rich purple depending on the selection. These hybrids are hardy in zones 4–10 and should be grown in sun.

There are eight different named Kosar/de Vos hybrids, and all are good garden plants for their different flower colors and plant sizes. We feel, however, that *Magnolia* 'Susan' is the most beautiful. It has the deepest purple-pink flowers of the eight "Little Girls." The tepals are thin and twisted, looking like brilliant purple dragonflies in spring. The flowers have an excellent cinnamon and lemon scent and bloom sporadically over spring and summer.

If you want a magnolia collection, we can heartily recommend all the Kosar/de Vos hybrids. However, since most of these hybrids are similar, you might be better off trying other *Magnolia* species or hybrids for a longer season of bloom.

Magnolia liliiflora (lily magnolia). This Chinese species has been in Western gardens for two hundred years and was one of the first magnolias we planted in 1951. We still have

Magnolia liliiflora.

our original plant trained as a bonsai in our garden. It is normally a multistemmed 15-foot (4.6 m) shrub. Its dark green leaves are glossy as they emerge but develop more of a matte surface later in summer. The flowers are 3–4 inches (7.5–10 cm) across, dark purple outside, and almost white inside. The tepals are sharply pointed and very upright. The main bloom time is early spring, but *M. liliiflora* and all of its hybrids flower sporadically all summer.

Magnolia liliiflora 'O'Neill'. A superb small magnolia for gardens of any size. It was developed by the late Joe McDaniel of the University of Illinois at Urbana-Champaign, who was a leading proponent of magnolias and one of the founders of the Magnolia Society. This shrubby plant grows up to 15 feet (4.6 m) tall in thirty years. Ours has fifteen to twenty trunks and makes a bushy shrub. The deep green leaves have a glossy surface all summer and are much larger and broader than those of the species. In early spring 'O'Neill' is covered with large, 6- to 8-inch (15 cm to 20 cm), broad-tepaled flowers with a rich, deep purple exterior and lighter purple interior. They have a sweet cinnamon-lemon fragrance. This selection has an amazingly long bloom period, with open flowers as well as very small buds from the beginning of the bloom season. Our plant blooms for at least a month. If this shrub is hit by frost while in bloom, its flowers will continue to open later in the season. Hardy in zones 4–10. Grow in sun.

Magnolia liliiflora 'O'Neill'.

Magnolia sieboldii. A Japanese species with some of the most beautiful flowers of any magnolia. This 15- to 20-foot (4.6 m to 6 m) plant grows in an open vase shape. As it gets older it develops a more horizontal form, displaying the flowers even more beautifully. The leaves are oval and about 6 inches (15 cm) long, appearing in midspring and dropping by very early fall. The flowers appear from late spring to midsummer, blooming continually through the season. The buds

Magnolia sieboldii.

look like small white eggs hanging from the tree. When they open, the pendulous flowers are white with deep red-maroon stamens, carrying a wonderful scent like tropical fruits. *Magnolia sieboldii* is best planted on a mound or above a path so that you can look up into the beautiful flowers and see the little, bright pink fruits that appear in late summer. It should be grown in afternoon shade so that its thin bark doesn't sunburn. Our plant grows in full sun, but we let the branches and foliage grow all the way to the ground to protect the bark. Hardy in zones 6–9.

Magnolia stellata (star magnolia). This excellent flowering shrub from Japan is almost too universally known to require an introduction. It can be seen in an enormous range of climates and gardens, growing to 20–25 feet (6–7.6 m) tall in as many years, although some of our plants are forty years old and with only minor pruning have only become 15 feet (4.6 m) tall and 8 feet (2.4 m) wide. This magnolia can be a single-trunked small tree, or its many stems can be pruned to form a shrubby plant. The foliage is deep green and full, appearing in early spring. The leaves are 3–4 inches (7.5–10 cm) long and about 1 inch (2.5 cm) wide. The flowers can have six to eight tepals, or as many as sixty in some of the double forms such as *M. stellata* 'Jane Platt'. The flowers are 3–4 inches (7.5–10 cm) across and either light pink or white in early spring. Hardy in zones 5–9. Grow in sun.

Magnolia stellata 'Jane Platt'. This is one of only four or five different plants we have named after several decades of gardening. We first saw this beautiful magnolia in Jane and John Platt's glorious garden in the 1970s. Mrs. Platt was incredibly generous and gave us cuttings to root. As our plant matured, we became increasingly impressed with the lovely pink flowers, which are 3–4 inches (7.5–10 cm) across and light pink from the time the buds open until the tepals fall off. We have counted more than sixty tepals on some flowers. After many years of growing this plant as *M. stellata* 'Rosea', we asked Mrs. Platt what she would like it to be named. Very uncharacteristically, she said,

"How about 'Jane Platt'?" We named it just that, and dedicated our catalog to her that fall. She never said anything to us, but we heard she was thrilled. When 'Jane Platt' was exhibited at the Royal Horticultural Society, it received an Award of Merit, a thrill to Mr. Platt and our family. Hardy in zones 5–10. Grow in sun.

Magnolia stellata 'Royal Star'. The standard *M. stellata* in the nursery industry. If you go to a nursery anywhere in the country and ask for this species, you will most likely be sold 'Royal Star'. Nonetheless, the fact that this cultivar is common isn't a reason to scoff at it. This seedling was found by the Vermeulen

Magnolia stellata 'Jane Platt'.

Nursery of Neshanic Station, New Jersey, and named in the 1950s. It is a seedling of *M. stellata* 'Waterlily'. The white flowers are 3–4 inches (7.5–10 cm) across, and there are twenty-five to thirty tepals. Blooms cover the plant in early spring. If you are looking for a consistently good-quality star magnolia, 'Royal Star' will fit the bill. Hardy in zones 5–10.

Magnolia stellata 'Waterlily'. Four slightly different clones are grown under this name, all of them good plants. The flower buds start out pink and fade to white with a pinkish tinge. There are fourteen to twenty tepals in a flower 3–4 inches (7.5–10 cm) wide. Our form blooms at the stem ends as well as in the axils. Michael Dirr says this cultivar blooms consistently later than *M. stellata* 'Royal Star', but our plants bloom at the same time (perhaps we have a different clone?). Hardy in zones 5–10. Grow in sun.

Mahonia

These members of the barberry family flower in fall, winter, or early spring, making them very important garden plants. They all have spiny leaves, but the stems don't have spines as barberries do. The plants range from 1-foot (0.3 m) creeping ground covers to 20-foot (6 m) spectacular shrubs, with evergreen foliage that can be dark green, purplish gray-green, or peachy orange depending on the species or time of year. Different mahonias have leaves of various sizes and with varying amounts of spines. For years we didn't grow mahonias or barberries because of the thorns and spines, but we eventually found

that their great foliage, flowers, and forms are worth the effort. The flowers appear any time after early fall and bloom on different species until midspring. Generally the flowers are in terminal clusters that are bright yellow, but a few mahonias, such as *M. gracilipes*, have copper-colored flowers.

These shrubs seem to be very adaptable to a variety of growing conditions. Our native *Mahonia aquifolium* is frequently planted in compacted soil in parking lots and around commercial buildings where it sits in water all winter. We can't imagine how a plant might do if it was cared for.

Origin: Western United States, south-
eastern Asia.
Hardiness: Zones 5–10.
Exposure: Sun to partial shade.

Mahonia bealei. This Chinese species is a hardy, heavy-stemmed grower to 6 feet (1.8 m) tall. The leaves are large and coarse. The flowers appear in early spring in large, upright, yellow trusses and have a wonderful lily of the valley scent. Roger remembers encountering *M. bealei* in the late 1970s, and the fragrance instantly brings back memories of spring. Hardy in zones 5–9. Grow in partial shade.

Mahonia ×media. This cross between *M. japonica* and *M. lomariifolia* represents one of the greatest groups of plants selected for the woodland garden in the twentieth century. Over time, these fast-growing evergreen shrubs can get to be really large, up to 20 feet (6 m) tall—our plant of *M. ×media* 'Winter Sun' is 16 feet (4.9 m) tall after twenty years—but whatever space you give them will reward you every year. They are multistemmed and upright, especially in lots of sunlight; in shade they can open up and become more horizontal. Some forms of *M. ×media* are truly fall blooming, while others are winter blooming. Some have upright racemes, and others have drooping racemes. All have large, yellow, sweetly fragrant racemes, and all are glorious. The fruit appears in spring as green pearls that turn purple. As soon as the fruit changes color, flocks of cedar waxwings come and eat every one. All *M. ×media* hybrids are excellent for their different attributes. Picking a favorite would be tough: we like all of them. Hardy in zones 6–10.

***Mahonia ×media* 'Charity'.** This is the most commonly available variety, a cultivar with drooping racemes in late fall. The leaves are up to 18 inches (45 cm) long and are at their most extraordinary when provided more shade. Grow in sun to partial shade.

Mahonia nervosa (Cascade Oregon grape, dwarf Oregon grape). Native to the Coast Range and Cascades, this creeping shrub is amazingly adaptable in gardens or native situations. It makes a suckering shrub up to 3

Mahonia ×media 'Charity'.

feet (0.9 m) tall depending on whether it is grown in sun or shade (in shade it grows to 2–3 feet [0.6–0.9 m], in full sun to only 1 foot [0.3 m]). This plant isn't a full grower but rather an open suckering shrub that can be grown with other ground covers or native plants. The foliage is dark green through spring and summer, deep purple-red through fall and winter; it looks like a small form of the typical *Mahonia* and grows upright out of the root stalk. The flowers are bright yellow in early to midspring and are much shorter than most of the other *Mahonia* species we've seen. *Mahonia nervosa* isn't as showy as many other mahonias but can be a good woodland or full-sun grower for the garden. It is hardy in zones 4–9.

Gardeners don't always fully appreciate the plants native to their own region. We remember seeing *Mahonia nervosa* in Princess Sturdza's Le Vasterival, a garden in France. The princess had bought the plant in England and kept it protected within a cage.

Osmanthus (tea olive)

These relatives of the olive look very much like hollies, but the leaves are opposite rather than alternate. They range in size from small shrubs to small trees. We've seen plants of *O. yunnanensis* that are 20 feet (6 m) tall. All forms of *Osmanthus* have evergreen foliage, and some are prickly like hollies, while others have finely serrated leaves. Most have deep green leaves, but some cultivars are splashed with other colors on the leaf blade or margin, and at least one has golden yellow foliage.

Origin: Japan.

Hardiness: Zones 7–10.
Exposure: Partial shade.

Osmanthus ×fortunei 'San Jose'. This cultivar has been grown at Hendricks Park in Eugene, Oregon, since the 1950s. In 1972, temperatures in our region dropped to –12°F (–24°C), and though our plants of 'San Jose' were damaged, they proved hardy and came back quickly. This upright evergreen gets too large over time to be entirely appropriate for this book, but it is too good a plant to be ignored. The small white flowers, which are held in clusters along the stems, carry the fragrance of apricots through the garden each fall. But even if 'San Jose' didn't bloom, it would be well worth growing just for its foliage and form. It makes a great large-scale hedge and, with growth up to 18 inches (45 cm) a year, can be used for screening unwanted eyesores fairly quickly. The deep green 3- to 4-inch (7.5 cm to 10 cm) leaves have soft prickles along the margin. Hardy in zones 6–10. Grow in sun to shade.

Osmanthus fragrans. This upright Chinese species reportedly reaches 20–25 feet (6–7.6 m) tall, though we have only seen 8- to 10-foot (2.4 m to 3 m) plants. The foliage is deep green and very leathery. Our plants have been damaged by deep freezes, their leaves falling off when the temperature dropped to 0°F (–18°C). The orange-yellow flowers bloom in late fall and are incredibly fragrant, smelling of apricots. We remember noticing the scent of *O. fragrans* at the Portland Classical Chinese Garden from a block away. When grown in western Washington, Oregon, or the Deep South, this plant makes a distinctive statement in the fall garden. Hardy in zones 7–10. Grow in partial shade.

Osmanthus heterophyllus 'Goshiki'. Introduced and named at Brookside Gardens in Maryland, this mound-shaped, variegated plant grows to 6 feet (1.8 m) tall. In spring the evergreen foliage is yellow or light green with flecks of gold, maturing to dark green with gold splashes. We don't usually like splashed variegation, but this cultivar's foliage is beautiful. Hardy in zones 6–10. Grow in sun to partial shade.

Osmanthus heterophyllus 'Ogon'. This is one of the finest yellow-foliaged evergreen plants we grow, its leaves a brilliant golden yellow year-round. It took us a long time to discover where it wants to grow. Our plant tends to burn and underperform in full sun and grows best in all-day shade. Hardy in zones 6–10.

Osmanthus heterophyllus 'Sasaba'. As Michael Dirr says, this cultivar is the plant handler's nightmare. An upright grower, it reaches 6–8 feet (1.8–2.4 m) tall and only 2 feet (0.6 m) wide. In our experience it is slow growing, and since a three-year-old plant will be just 6 inches (15 cm) tall, it can be difficult to get people to try growing it. The very narrow, deeply lobed, deep green leaves have a sharp spine at the tip, but as with barberries, once 'Sasaba' is planted the thorns are not a problem. We first saw this shrub at Brookside Gardens and thought the form and foliage were very attractive. Hardy in zones 6–10. Grow in partial shade.

Paeonia

The tree peonies or truly shrubby peonies are, in short, spectacular. They are slow growers, reaching perhaps 5–6 feet (1.5–1.8 m) tall in time. Their thick stems usually branch from below the soil line, forming a multitrunked shrub. The foliage is deeply pinnately cut and can be almost tropical looking from spring through fall. These peonies are so distinctive that in the garden their foliage can't be missed. Many have beautiful red-orange and yellow fall color.

Tree peonies need to have good drainage and full sun to partial shade. Our plants are in full sun all morning and semishade by early afternoon. We have chosen to include mostly hybrids bred in the United States. We like the rich colors and more elegant, single to semidouble flowers that set these tree peonies apart from others we have seen.

Origin: China.
Hardiness: Zones 4–8.
Exposure: Sun to partial shade.

Paeonia 'Alhambra'. The large, ruffled flowers of this A. P. Saunders hybrid are golden yellow in midspring. Because it is both beautiful and a quick, easy grower, we recommend 'Alhambra' for the beginning grower. Hardy in zones 4–8.

Paeonia 'Black Panther'. Another A. P. Saunders hybrid. The large, deep purple-red flowers that appear in midspring have a glossy sheen. The foliage is deeply cut, creating an excellent frame for the flowers. Hardy in zones 4–8. Grow in sun.

Paeonia 'Gauguin'. It's hard to say too much about such a glorious flower. In midspring the large flowers are a mixture of purple highlights on peach and pink, a color combination that doesn't sound nearly as beautiful as these flowers actually are. The flowers change color every day but are lovely all through the bloom season. Hardy in zones 4–8. Grow in sun.

Paeonia 'Leda'. The huge, deep pink, single to semidouble flowers of this Nassos Daphnis hybrid appear in midspring and have a light, pleasant fragrance. The first plant we saw with this unreal pink flower was only 1 foot (0.3 m) tall. Hardy in zones 4–8. Grow in sun.

Paeonia rockii (Joseph Rock tree peony, Rock's variety tree peony). This peony, which we have read is a hybrid, was found in a monastery garden in China. Its huge white buds are like goose eggs that get more and more voluptuous before they open. The flowers are white, probably 8–10 inches (20–25 cm) across, and single to semidouble; they would be impressive enough if that were all, but there are also deep purple spots at the base of the petals. *Paeonia rockii* isn't easy to find and is very expensive. Even though it is easy to grow, it is very difficult to graft and doesn't produce much scion wood. For these reasons it will probably always be scarce, but keep after it, because this amazing plant is

Paeonia rockii flower and buds.

worth the effort. Hardy in zones 4–8. Grow in sun.

Philadelphus (mock orange)

These deciduous shrubs have been in gardens throughout temperate Europe and America for hundreds of years. Their flowers are so beautiful and so sweetly citrus-scented, how could we not grow them? Plants range in size from only 4–5 feet (1.2–1.5 m) tall up to 15 feet (4.6 m) depending on the species or hybrid. They have multiple trunks and need some thinning to create an attractive form. The leaves, which are ovate and small (2 inches [5 cm]), give the plant a fine texture. There are golden and variegated forms of some of the species, offering more seasonal interest. The bloom season isn't long, but many of the cultivars have lovely white flowers. The flowers are all single to double and appear in early summer. On a few mock oranges, there is a lavender to purple flush inside the flowers. When Eric and Roger's grandmother was married in July 1923, her wedding bouquet was made of our native mock orange.

Origin: Europe, Asia, North America.
Hardiness: Zones 5–10.
Exposure: Sun to partial shade.

Philadelphus 'Belle Etoile'. This hybrid from France is one of our favorite mock oranges. When we first heard about it in the 1980s, we ordered it from several nurseries, but all the plants we received were mislabeled—we were sent singles, doubles, and everything in between. We finally found that Glenn Withey and Charles Price had a large specimen in Seattle; they had bought a plant in the late 1950s from the old Wayside Gardens in Ohio. We received plants from this source through Phillip Curtis Farms in Canby, Oregon, an excellent small wholesale nursery from 1986 until about 2000. This goes to show how difficult it is to track down the correct plant. 'Belle Etoile' is a 10- to 12-foot (3 m to 3.6 m) shrub with a fairly open habit. The medium green leaves are 2–3 inches (5–7.5 cm) long and ½ inch (1.25 cm) wide. The 2-inch (5 cm) flowers are pure sparkling white with a light purple blush on the inside of the petals. The flowers appear in late spring to early summer and are very fragrant. In warmer climates the purple blush will fade, but because the flowers and fragrance are so nice, this selection is well worth growing. Hardy in zones 4–8. Grow in sun to partial shade.

Philadelphus coronarius. This species originated in Italy, Romania, and Austria and has been grown for generations. It is very bushy because of its multiple stems. We have grown it for twenty years and don't need to thin our plants for disease prevention, though we presume it would be best to thin in more humid climates.

Philadelphus coronarius 'Aureus'. The main feature of this moderate 6- to 8-foot (1.8 m to 2.4 m) grower is its small (1- to 2-inch [2.5 cm to 5 cm]), brilliant golden yellow leaves, which cover the plant thickly from spring until fall. The flowers are strongly scented from late spring to early summer but are also small and sparingly borne. A very good plant

Philadelphus coronarius 'Aureus'.

for its shock of color in spring and summer. It needs some afternoon shade to keep from burning. Hardy in zones 4–8.

Philadelphus coronarius 'Variegatus'. This good, small-growing, variegated shrub is rarely seen in gardens. Its green leaves have broad creamy white margins. We have only seen small plants that are 2–3 feet (0.6–0.9 m) tall. Like *P. coronarius* 'Aureus', this cultivar flowers only sparsely and needs some afternoon shade. Hardy in zones 4–8.

Physocarpus opulifolius (ninebark)
This multitrunked shrub reaches 8–12 feet (2.4–3.6 m) tall. As a young plant it grows in an upright vase shape, maturing into a broad, arching, graceful shrub. The deep green leaves are about 2 inches (5 cm) long with three deep lobes. The fall color isn't great but can be a nice yellow. Small, white, spiraea-like flowers appear in clusters in midspring and are attractive but not really showy.

In 1992 Graham Stuart Thomas wrote in his superb *Ornamental Shrubs, Climbers, and*

Bamboos that "*Physocarpus* are not in the first flight of ornamental shrubs, tending to take up more space than they deserve." Things have changed. We now have a range of varieties offering a real splash of foliage color.

Origin: Eastern United States.

Hardiness: Zones 2–9.

Exposure: Sun to partial shade.

Physocarpus opulifolius Coppertina ('Mindia'). The newest ninebark to our garden, this hybrid by Minier Nursery of France has many great aspects to recommend it. It is a cross of *P. opulifolius* 'Dart's Gold' and *P. opulifolius* 'Diabolo' and shares some of the colors of both parents. The foliage is coppery in spring, with a yellow flush to the center of the leaf, and reddish purple in summer. The flowers are the typical clusters of white in midspring. Like all physocarpus, this cultivar is an easy grower in full sun to partial shade and can take quite a bit of drought. Hardy in zones 2–9.

Physocarpus opulifolius 'Dart's Gold'. This large, golden-leaved ninebark was around when Graham Stuart Thomas wrote his book. It is smaller than *P. opulifolius* 'Luteus'. The leaves are brilliant yellow in spring and early summer, light greenish yellow by midsummer, and butter yellow in fall. Hardy in zones 2–9. Grow in sun.

Physocarpus opulifolius 'Diabolo'. This beautiful purple-leaved plant appeared in American horticulture in the 1980s–1990s. It is an excellent plant for either the perennial border or the shrub border. The leaves are a good backdrop for the clusters of light pinkish flowers that appear in midspring. We use 'Diabolo' as a background for pink, purple, or white flowers, and it would make a great host for a small-flowered vine. We also grow it as an understory for *Catalpa bignonioides* 'Aurea', an exciting combination. It's amazing how fast some plants have been improved by clever nurseries and hybridizers. Hardy in zones 2–9. Grow in sun.

Pieris (lily of the valley shrub)

These great, medium-sized, evergreen shrubs are grown almost as much as *Rhododendron* hybrids, especially in the Pacific Northwest and other milder-weather areas. They are densely bushy with narrow, glossy foliage and can eventually reach the eaves of a house. The flower buds can be very attractive from fall until spring, and the white to dark red flowers appear in early spring as drooping sprays.

These easy-to-grow plants need the same conditions as rhododendrons, namely well-drained, moist soil. Their only problem, which we rarely see, is spider mite damage on the foliage in late summer. They can be grown in either semishade or full sun, as long as it's not a reflected south-facing site.

Origin: Japan.

Hardiness: Zones 6–9.

Exposure: Partial shade or full sun.

Pieris 'Bert Chandler'. An Australian selection grown for its brilliant pink new growth in spring, which continues to change as it ages, transitioning to soft yellow and eventually to light green. Though shy to flower, this cultivar is well worth growing for its attractive foliage. Hardy in zones 7–9. Grow in partial shade.

Pieris 'Flaming Silver'. We first saw this fine cultivar, which is probably a hybrid of *P. formosa* and *P. japonica*, listed in Holland in the early 1980s. The foliage is evergreen, with shrimp pink new growth emerging in early spring over the previous year's deep green leaves margined by creamy white. As spring continues, the pink foliage changes until it eventually takes on the green and white var-iegation. Our plants have been hit by frost during new growth and within two or three weeks pushed a new set of leaves. Hardy in zones 7–9. Grow in partial shade.

Pieris japonica 'Little Heath'. Roger first saw this cultivar in 1990 in England, but it took a while to find plants in Holland. We received two or three small plants, all of which survived the importation. We eventually put one in the garden, and it is now over 5 feet (1.5 m) tall, although most references

Pieris 'Flaming Silver'.

describe 'Little Heath' as growing to 3 feet (0.9 m) tall. The leaves are small, 1½ inches (4 cm) long and ½ inch (1.25 cm) wide, and medium green with a creamy white margin. The flowers are only sporadically produced, but the foliage and form of this plant make it well worth growing. It will revert to a green leaf off and on. Some people grow *P. japonica* 'Little Heath Green', which to our eyes is nothing more than a green blob; it, too, flowers sparsely. Hardy in zones 6–9. Grow in partial shade.

Pieris japonica 'Valley Valentine'. A selection from Bob Tichnor's breeding program at Oregon State University's North Willamette Research and Extension Center. This 6- to 8-foot (1.8 m to 2.4 m) shrub has been around since the 1960s and is still one of the finest red-flowering forms of *Pieris*. The evergreen, glossy, deep green foliage makes a perfect backdrop for the deep red-purple buds in winter. Red flowers appear in spring in large, drooping clusters. This easy grower makes an attractive complement to any gar-

Pieris japonica 'Little Heath'.

The red, drooping flower clusters of *Pieris japonica* 'Valley Valentine'.

den year-round. Hardy in zones 6–9. Grow in partial shade.

Poncirus trifoliata (hardy orange)

This is a weird plant. The irregular habit of its deep green stems, which eventually form a small 15- to 20-foot (4.6 m to 6 m) tree or large shrub, makes it more curious than beautiful. If you want a hedge that no one will ever try to get through, this is it—we have even heard rumor that one of the barriers at Fort Knox is a hedge of *P. trifoliata*. And this is without even having mentioned the thorns. The word *thorns* is an understatement: these 2-inch (5 cm) spines are hard and woody, adding to this plant's impenetrability. The leaves are deep green, fairly small, deciduous, and sparse. The flowers are citrus-scented and about 2 inches (5 cm) across in spring. They are followed by small, irregular, yellow, sour fruit.

Origin: China.
Hardiness: Zones 5–9.
Exposure: Sun.

Poncirus trifoliata 'Flying Dragon'. This demented plant is only for the garden sadist. Everything is contorted on it—stems, leaves, flowers, fruit—and you must be careful to avoid getting caught in the thorns. It is a wonderful container plant, however, because it is slow to grow, and it makes quite a statement.

Rhamnus frangula 'Asplenifolia'

This very hardy shrub can grow to 15 feet (4.6 m) tall and 10 feet (3 m) wide after twenty years. The species has an oval leaf, but 'Asplenifolia' has a long, very narrow leaf—on our plants, 4–5 inches (10–12.5 cm) long and only ½ inch (1.25 cm) wide. The fine-textured, somewhat bamboo-like foliage is deep green from spring through summer, turning a nice golden yellow in fall. The stems are dark gray with small white spots, so even in winter 'Asplenifolia' has an interesting color and form. Drought resistant and easy to grow.

Origin: Europe.
Hardiness: Zones 3–7.
Exposure: Sun.

Rhamnus frangula Fine Line ('Ron Williams')

This plant makes a very narrow silhouette, reaching 8–10 feet (20–25 cm) tall and about 1 foot (0.3 m) wide. We like the idea of a columnar deciduous shrub, but the small plants

The fine-textured, green foliage of *Rhamnus frangula* 'Asplenifolia'.

In fall *Rhamnus frangula* 'Asplenifolia' turns golden yellow.

we have seen lack the grace of *R. frangula* 'Asplenifolia'. We have planted a small specimen in our garden to see whether Fine Line will live up to its hype.

Origin: Europe.
Hardiness: Zones 3–7.
Exposure: Sun.

Rhododendron

Where to begin or end with this ubiquitous group of plants? These beautiful flowering shrubs can be grown from Southern California and Florida, where azaleas do especially well, all the way to Canada, where you can find the superhardy rhododendrons. In the Pacific Northwest, where rhododendrons are almost too easy to grow, they become small trees, covering windows and eventually outgrowing all but the largest garden.

Rhododendrons were very popular from the 1940s through the 1980s and during that time were overplanted in many gardens. But plants, like most other things, go in and out of fashion, and many gardeners now refuse to plant them. What a pity, for these are stunning plants.

We have traditionally grown species rhododendrons, mostly from China and Japan, rather than the hybrids. In the early 1960s we became interested in the species for their beautiful foliage and flowers. In fact we brought all the plants for the Rhododendron Species Foundation (now in Federal Way, Washington) to Eugene from Vancouver, British Columbia, in the late 1960s.

Rhododendron species come in a variety of sizes. They can grow as ground covers that will follow the cracks in the rocks and eventually get to 2 inches (5 cm) tall. A twenty-year-old plant of *R. calostrotum* subsp. *keleticum* that we grew occupied a space of 4 inches (10 cm) by 6 inches (15 cm) and was all of 1 inch (2.5 cm) tall. On the opposite end of the scale is *R. arboreum*, which develops into an 80-foot (24 m) tree over time in areas where it is native.

Rhododendron foliage can be among the finest of any shrub that can be grown. There are both evergreen and deciduous species, with leaves ranging from ½ inch (1.25 cm) long all the way to 24 inches (61 cm) long.

The flowers appear in showy trusses that can be white, pink, yellow, orange, red-purple, or almost black. The trusses adorn the plant (depending on the species) any time from late winter until midsummer. For the most part we grow rhododendrons as foliage plants, but some listed here also have beautiful flowers.

Origin: China, Japan, Southeast Asia.

Hardiness: Zones 5–9.

Exposure: Partial shade.

Rhododendron albrechtii. This deciduous Japanese native forms an open shrub to 6 feet (1.8 m) tall in as many years. In early spring the glowing purple-pink flowers decorate the leafless plant. We remember seeing plants at Jane Platt's garden that had the flat-petaled flowers distributed all over them. The flower color is such a glowing shade of purple that it

Rhododendron albrechtii.

almost pulses like a butterfly. We are hoping that our listing will encourage more people to call for some of these deciduous azaleas. Hardy in zones 5–8. Grow in partial shade.

Rhododendron argyrophyllum subsp. ***nankingense*** 'Chinese Silver'. An upright grower from Sichuan Province, China, that eventually reaches 12–15 feet (3.6–4.6 m) tall. We had a plant that was 12 feet (3.6 m) tall and 6 feet (1.8 m) wide. The stiff, leathery, deeply veined leaves are deep green year-round with a silver sheen underneath. The midspring flowers are small, rich pink bells that make a beautiful ornament above the dark green leaves. Plant in filtered shade to protect the foliage from burning. Hardy in zones 6–8.

Rhododendron bureavii. This 6-foot (1.8 m) shrub from Yunnan Province, China, is covered with deep green leaves that have rusty-colored indumentum underneath year-round. The flowers are soft pink to white in midspring. Provide some afternoon shade to prevent sunburn. Hardy in zones 7–8.

Rhododendron kiusianum. A deciduous Japanese azalea that can get up to 2 feet (0.6 m) tall in time. The leaves are small (½ inch [1.25 cm]) and deep green from spring to fall, with some remaining on the plant through mild winters. In spring the plant leafs out, then is covered with pink flowers that are white at the center. Selections are available in many different colors for almost any spring garden.

Rhododendron argyrophyllum subsp. *nankingense* 'Chinese Silver'.

Very easy to grow in full sun to semishade. Hardy in zones 5–9.

Rhododendron lutescens. This Chinese species has about everything you could want in a garden plant. The narrow foliage is bronze in spring, becoming dark green with some purplish highlights. The bright yellow 2-inch (5 cm) flowers are held in clusters, with only two or three flowers per truss, and are a perfect match with the new growth. This upright shrub needs a little shade and protection from spring frost, which can damage the flowers and young leaves. Hardy in zones 7–8.

Rhododendron macabeanum. This Chinese species is one of the big-leaved rhododendrons, though its leaves are not among the

The undersides of *Rhododendron macabeanum* leaves have a white indumentum.

largest of the lot, and in the wild it can get to be the size of a small tree. The stiff, large stems make a sturdy frame for the large, oval, evergreen leaves, which are dark green with deep veining on top and white indumentum underneath. The flowers can take a while to appear. In fact our original plant took thirty-five years to bloom! The plant had grown to 6 feet (1.8 m) when it was frozen at –12°F (–24°C). Deciding it was dead, we took it to the compost pile. That summer we saw that it was growing, so we took pity and brought it back to the garden, where it grew beautifully. It seemed ready to bloom but was frozen again when the temperature twice dropped to 0°F (–18°C), but it grew back and finally, after several years, bloomed for a month. The large, golden yellow, bell-shaped flowers are formed into an upright truss. The flowers are glorious, but we also appreciated the beautiful foliage during all those years. *Rhododendron macabeanum* is a plant for the young at heart or the very optimistic. Hardy in zones 7–9. Grow in partial shade.

Rhododendron orbiculare. The midgreen leaves of this species are almost round, as the name states, and are held to the stem by purple petioles. The deep pink, bell-like flowers appear in midspring in a loose truss. This 6-foot (1.8 m), rounded shrub from Sichuan Province, China, is lovely in the garden any time of year. Hardy in zones 7–9. Grow in partial shade.

Rhododendron proteoides. This native of Tibet and Yunnan Province, China, is among the true tiny treasures of the rhododendron family. The most famous plant we ever saw was in a stump at Cecil Smith's lovely woodland rhododendron garden in Newberg, Oregon. Our original plant was put in the ground in the early 1970s and is now 8 inches (20 cm) tall and 12 inches (30 cm) wide. The leaves are ½ inch (1.25 cm) long, ¼ inch (0.6 cm) wide, and deep green, with a rusty indumentum underneath. This exceptional dwarf rhododendron has small clusters of pink and white flowers that add just a little more zip in midspring. The soil must be well drained year-round, and it's best to grow *R. proteoides* in semishade. Hardy in zones 7–8.

Rhododendron pseudochrysanthum. This Taiwanese native was fairly rare until the late 1980s. Depending on the form, it can be 2–6 feet (0.6–1.8 m) tall. The very stiff, evergreen leaves are 2–3 inches (5–7.5 cm) long and 1 inch (2.5 cm) across. New leaves have a silver tomentum through much of spring and summer. Although this plant is incredibly attractive just for its foliage, it offers small trusses of apple blossom pink and white flowers. *Rhododendron pseudochrysanthum* is also the parent of many lovely hybrids, the best of which is *R.* 'Golfer'. Hardy in zones 6–9. Grow in partial shade.

Rhododendron recurvoides. This slow-growing rhododendron from northern Myanmar is the Rolls-Royce of rhododendrons, according to Harold Greer, past president of the American Rhododendron Society. It slowly grows to 4 feet (1.2 m) of mounded foliage. The leaves are deep forest green with a beautiful rusty indumentum. *Rhododendron* *recurvoides* is one of the most beautiful foliage plants available (among rhododendrons or any other plant). The white flowers have some pink markings and sometimes pinkish purple spots on the interior. Hardy in zones 6–8. Grow in partial shade.

Rhododendron roxieanum var. oreonastes. This upright grower to 5 feet (1.5 m) tall is native to Yunnan Province and Tibet. It is much more upright than *R. recurvoides*. The very narrow leaves are 3–4 inches (7.5–10 cm) long and ½ inch (1.25 cm) wide, and deep green with a dusty orangish indumentum. The flowers are typical of the *Taliense* series in that they are pink-white and fairly small. This variety is a superb foliage plant for the woodland garden. Hardy in zones 6–8. Grow in partial shade.

Rhododendron schlippenbachii (royal azalea). A deciduous Japanese azalea of regal beauty that can get to 8–10 feet (20–25 cm) tall in thirty years. The leaves are fairly thin and can burn in sun, so this plant should be in filtered shade most of the day. The oval leaves emerge in early spring with a slight purplish cast, turning an attractive buttery yellow in fall. The flowers can be white through medium pink depending on the seedling or selection. For instance, *R. schlippenbachii* 'Sid's Royal Pink' is rich pink. The flowers are borne on the leafless branches, so they show up beautifully. Hardy in zones 6–9.

Rhododendron williamsianum. This native of Sichuan Province, China, is a slow-growing mound of foliage, and although that description doesn't sound too attractive, in reality this is a beautiful foliage plant. We remember seeing pictures of very old plants in England that were 6 feet (1.8 m) tall and 10 feet (3 m) wide. We have had a plant of *R. williamsianum* that was grafted as a standard in the late 1970s by Art Wright in Canby, Oregon. The plant is 3 feet (0.9 m) tall and 2 feet (0.6 m) wide. The leaves are only 1–1½ inches (2.5–4 cm) wide and perfectly oval, lying plastered against each other so that no branches show. They are bronze in spring, turning deep green later in the season. The soft, light pink, bell-like flowers are really beautiful but very shyly borne. On a grafted plant like our standard, the flowers are so heavily presented that the leaves barely show. We don't know why the cuttings don't have the heavy blooming of the grafted plants, but even without any flowers *R. williamsianum* is a lovely plant year-round. Hardy in zones 6–9. Grow in partial shade.

Rhododendron yakushimanum. This Japanese species has everything: a beautiful mounding form, glorious deep green leaves, attractive pink-white blooms, and enough hardiness to grow throughout much of the United States. It comes from the island of Yaku Shima, Japan, on which the coastal areas are subtropical and the highest points are alpine. *Rhododendron yakushimanum* varies greatly in height and spread. We have dwarf forms that are 2 feet (0.6 m) tall and 3 feet (0.9 m) wide after forty years. We also have one plant that is 10–12 feet (3–3.6 m) tall and 12 feet (3.6 m) wide. The leaves are narrow and dark green year-round with very

Opposite top: *Rhododendron yakushimanum*.

Opposite bottom: A collection of *Rhododendron yakushimanum* seedlings shows the variation in foliage.

thick, fawn-colored indumentum. In late spring the new growth can be even more beautiful than the flowers, which are apple-blossom pink and white when they bloom in midspring. Some of the larger selections have really beautiful trusses in spring. Our plants all withstood a low of –12°F (–24°C) in 1972 without any—we repeat, *any*—kind of damage, and *R. yakushimanum* is said to endure temperatures as low as –20°F (–29°C) on down to –30°F (–34°C). Hardy in zones 5–9. Grow in sun to partial shade.

Rhododendron yakushimanum 'Koichiro Wada'. Named for the late super plantsman from Japan, this smaller form only reaches 2–3 feet (0.6–0.9 m) tall and makes a superb mounding shrub. The convex leaves are deep

Because of its size, *Rhododendron yakushimanum* 'Koichiro Wada', bottom left, combines well with low-growing perennials.

green, with a glossy sheen and excellent light tan indumentum. The light pink-white flowers are small but cover the plant when they appear in late spring.

Rhododendron yakushimanum 'Phetteplace'. The giant form of the species. Our plant is 12 feet (3.6 m) tall and at least 12 feet across after forty years. The large, soft pink flowers are very showy in spring. Hardy in zones 5–9. Grow in partial shade.

Ribes ×*gordonianum*

This cross between yellow *R. odoratum* and red *R. sanguineum* produces a lovely yellow to orangish flower with reddish highlights in early spring. Our plants are wider and shorter than *R. sanguineum*.

    Origin: Garden origin in Britain.
    Hardiness: Zones 4–9.
    Exposure: Sun.

Ribes sanguineum

This American currant is among the best flowering plants for the garden. People regularly ask us to identify it, and it always amazes us how a beautiful plant that grows naturally within a mile of our garden can remain so unknown. Ironically, we have seen plants of *R. sanguineum* growing in gardens and public spaces all over western France and England. It is not uncommon, however, to see our native plants more appreciated in Europe than they are at home.

    Ribes sanguineum grows in open woodland areas from central California clear through British Columbia. This fast-growing, trouble-free shrub can grow up to 8–10 feet (20–25

Opposite: Ribes sanguineum.

cm) tall in less than five years. We have had 2–3 feet (0.6–0.9 m) of growth on small plants. Though initially upright, *R. sanguineum* eventually spreads out and forms an irregular-growing shrub. The native plants are usually fairly slow growing and open in the wild. The deep green leaves resemble those of gooseberry (*Ribes uva-crispa*) and have a heavy, musty scent from spring through fall. The flowers are borne in racemes in early spring and can be white, pink, or red. Blossoms are produced even on small plants, so are a quick reward for planting. The various forms of *Ribes sanguineum* are perfect to plant with rhododendrons and magnolias because they bloom at the same times and add a burst of color.

    Origin: Western North America.
    Hardiness: Zones 5–10.
    Exposure: Sun to partial shade.

Ribes sanguineum 'Brocklebankii'. Our plant is more compact and slower growing than the other *R. sanguineum* cultivars. It would be beautiful with blue-flowered *Pulmonaria* 'Benediction'. The flowers are light pink and fairly insignificant in spring. Provide this plant with afternoon shade to protect the lovely golden foliage. Hardy in zones 5–7.

Ribes sanguineum 'Elk River Red'. This cultivar has been around the Portland area for many years and to us is the best red-flowered *R. sanguineum*. The racemes are wider and a little shorter than 'Pulborough Scarlet' but are

a true red and consistently produced. Hardy in zones 5–9. Grow in sun to partial shade.

Ribes sanguineum 'Pulborough Scarlet'. This cultivar has especially long, narrow racemes in early spring. The deep red flowers are very showy even on small plants. 'Pulborough Scarlet' grows very fast, so can put on a real show within just a couple years. It is probably the most commonly available form of *R. sanguineum* in nurseries and is well worth growing. Hardy in zones 5–9. Grow in sun to partial shade.

Ribes sanguineum White Icicle ('Ubric'). This form was named many years ago by the University of British Columbia Botanical Gar-

Ribes sanguineum 'Elk River Red'.

Ribes sanguineum White Icicle.

den and has shown how great a plant it is. We have grown it since the 1980s and really enjoy its large, sparkling white flowers in early spring. The foliage is lighter green than other cultivars during summer, but still attractive. Hardy in zones 5–9. Grow in sun to partial shade.

Rosa

Most gardeners grow hybrid teas, grandifloras, and old and new hybrids. We, however, are taken with the species, whose simple single flowers possess a grace the hybrids could only wish for.

We used to grow some of the old garden roses and loved the look and scent of the flowers, but we didn't enjoy staring at the bare stems after black spot or some other problem defoliated the plant. We don't use pesticides, so this was a challenge. Luckily we discovered species roses, which retain their leaves without the use of chemicals.

Origin: Northern Hemisphere.
Hardiness: Zones 5–9.
Exposure: Sun.

Rosa 'Geranium'. A Chinese native from Sichuan Province named at the Royal Horticultural Society's Wisley Garden in 1937 by the late Brian Mulligan, who later became director of Washington Park Arboretum in Seattle. This upright plant gets to be 6–8 feet (1.8–2.4 m) tall over several years. The leaves are pinnate and deep green through spring and fall. In early summer the single 3-inch (7.5 cm) flowers are "geranium red" (a really beautiful dusty red). 'Geranium' is worth growing for its attractive flowers alone, but its finest feature is its lovely hips, which are long, bottle-shaped, and bright orange-red in late summer to early fall. In *Trees and Shrubs*

Opposite top: *Rosa* 'Geranium' in flower.

Opposite bottom: Long orange-red hips appear on *Rosa* 'Geranium' in late summer to early fall.

Hardy in the British Isles, W. J. Bean wrote, "If there is room for only one *R. moyesii*, *R. geranium* should be chosen." Hardy in zones 6–9. Grow in sun.

Rosa glauca. This species from southern Europe is grown for its purple-gray leaves. It is a large shrub, getting up to 12 feet (3.6 m) tall, but many of the plants we have seen in gardens are 5–6 feet (1.5–1.8 m) tall due to regular pruning. When pruned, the foliage gets fuller and provides a superb background for all kinds of perennials, bulbs, and grasses. *Rosa glauca* blooms in early summer with

The brightly colored hips of *Rosa glauca*.

Rosa glauca has handsome purple-gray foliage and deep pink flowers.

small, 1- to 2-inch (2.5 cm to 5 cm), deep pink, single flowers followed by burnt orange hips in late summer or early fall. Our plants haven't been bothered by aphids, black spot, or any other problems after twenty years in the garden. Hardy in zones 2–9. Grow in sun.

Rosa rugosa. A native of Russia, northern China, Japan, and Korea, where it grows in sandy areas, usually by the sea, this thicket-forming (running, really) rose is incredibly drought resistant and hardy. An easy grower, it always looks attractive from spring to fall, reaching 4–5 feet (1.2–1.5 m) and forming a mounding plant with many stems growing from the ground. The stems have irregularly spaced thorns. Some forms have very few thorns, while others are covered with them. The leaves are deep green with veins that give a somewhat puckered appearance. The foliage looks healthy all summer and doesn't seem to attract any pests. The flowers are single or double and vary in color from pure white to deep reddish pink. Most cultivars are wonderfully scented and bloom sporadically through much of the summer. Orange-red hips are about 1 inch (2.5 cm) across and oval to round. We have had plants with flowers blooming a beautiful red at the same time as the hips.

All the cultivars and hybrids of *Rosa rugosa* that we have seen are good plants. Unfortunately we can't grow *R. rugosa* ourselves because this beautiful plant is much too happy and runs too quickly in our sandy loam soil. In contrast, clay soils will control the running, and if you want to garden in sand at the coast, *R. rugosa* will form a wonderful

large-scale ground cover. Hardy in zones 3–9. Grow in sun.

Rosa sericea subsp. **omeiensis** f. **pteracantha**. A rose that is grown for its thorns? True! This large shrub rose species from China has amazing, big, ruby red thorns from spring until midsummer. We have seen 15-foot (4.6

Rosa sericea subsp. *omeiensis* f. *pteracantha.*

m) plants in California that created the most incredible wind chimes in winter when the dried thorns clicked against each other. In spring and summer the deep green, pinnate leaves provide a good backdrop for the thorns, which are $^3/_4$ inch (1.9 cm) long and about $^1/_2$ inch (1.25 cm) high. The thorns show themselves best when the plant is situated to receive afternoon or early-morning sun; they are best seen with the sun behind them and look especially nice when the plant is wet. If you want to prolong the color of the thorns, try cutting back the plant by one-third in midsummer. It will regrow 12–18 inches (30–45 cm) by fall and show off the thorns to best effect. We prune (or butcher, as the case may be) our plants in late winter to about 18 inches (45 cm) to get the most regrowth during spring and summer. Because of this hard pruning, we don't get any of the small, single, white flowers in late spring, which isn't any loss. Hardy in zones 6–9.

Rubus 'Benenden'

A hybrid between *R. trilobus* and *R. deliciosus* from the great English plantsman Collingwood Ingram. When we were introduced to this wonderful blackberry by Reuben Hatch in the 1970s, we weren't sure if we wanted it. After all, Himalayan blackberry is one of the worst weeds in our area, the Pacific Coast, where it covers acres and spreads easily from seed. It turns out, however, that 'Benenden' is a totally safe blackberry. This 10-foot (3 m) open shrub has attractive, peeling, tan stems. It is deciduous, with deeply lobed, 2-inch (5 cm) leaves that are deep green all summer and golden yellow in fall. The open form of

this plant and its dark green leaves create a perfect backdrop for the single, pure white flowers, which are borne in early summer over at least a month. The crepe paper texture of the flowers along with the large center of yellow stamens makes a really beautiful display. 'Benenden' doesn't have thorns and is sterile, so it can't be spread by seeds. It is a shrub and can layer when branches touch the ground, but it will not spread beyond the garden and therefore makes an excellent shrub for either a watered garden or an unwatered woodland site.

Origin: Garden origin in Britain.
Hardiness: Zones 5–9.
Exposure: Partial shade.

Salix (willow)

The members of this large genus can be creeping subshrubs, magnificent trees, or any size in between. They can become fast-growing weedy species or incredibly difficult, slowgrowing plants. We will concentrate on the small growers and the small, multitrunked trees that can be cut back hard for their gorgeous winter stems.

Origin: Northern Hemisphere.
Hardiness: Zones 3–9.
Exposure: Sun.

***Salix alba* var. *sericea*.** This is a great large shrub or small tree to use as a substitute for *Pyrus salicifolia* 'Pendula' (weeping silver pear), which many gardeners see in person or in photographs from Sissinghurst Castle Garden in England. Although many people are entranced by the romance of the weeping silver pear, the problem is that it looks ugly in most gardens. It grows in the form of a haystack with unruly weeping stems. The stems have 1½-inch (4 cm) thorns and irregular silver leaves that are not very showy. The flowers are small, white, and very smelly. Enough said.

Salix alba var. *sericea* is by far the better choice. We have grown this willow as a large cut-back shrub and have seen it grown as a small tree. The stems are yellowish during winter and, though not exactly weeping, arch gracefully all summer. The leaves are light green as they emerge, remain gray-green all summer, and sometimes turn golden yellow in fall; they are narrow and long, ¼ inch (0.6 cm) by 4 inches (10 cm). All in all, *S. alba* var. *sericea* is easy to grow, easy to propagate, and provides the back of the border with a dash of silver. Grow in sun.

Salix alba var. vitellina 'Britzensis' (syn. *S. alba* 'Chermesina'). Native to Europe and northern Asia. This small tree has brilliant orange-red stems from fall to spring. We cut our plant down to 2–3 feet (0.6–0.9 m) at the same time the magnolias bloom in early

The colorful stems of *Salix alba* var. *vitellina* 'Britzensis'.

spring. It initially looks brutalized but quickly recovers and forms a 6- to 8-foot (1.8 m to 2.4 m) plant by fall. The leaves are narrow (½ inch [1.25 cm] wide and 4 inches [10 cm] long) and remain dark green all summer, turning a warm yellow in fall. The bright, shiny stems glow all winter. 'Britzensis' will grow in wet sites or well-drained areas. Hardy in zones 3–9. Grow in sun.

Salix fargesii. A Chinese willow that can get up to 10 feet (3 m) tall after many years. The stems are a rich mahogany through much of the year and can be rather attractive; they are thick and don't grow too fast each year—ours have grown about 1 foot (0.3 m) per year at the most. The leaves are deeply veined, leathery, and look almost evergreen. They are 6 inches (15 cm) long and 1½ inches (4 cm) wide, and vertical as they unfold out of the buds. The flowers are insignificant compared with the stems and leaves. *Salix fargesii* is beautiful combined with rhododendrons. Hardy in zones 6–9. Grow in well-drained soil in sun to partial shade.

Salix integra 'Hakuro-nishiki' (dappled willow). This variegated willow originated in Japan and Korea and eventually forms a large shrub up to about 15 feet (4.6 m) tall. In the

Opposite: *Salix integra* 'Hakuro-nishiki' can also be trained into a small tree, seen here at Schreiner's Iris Gardens in Salem, Oregon.

Salix integra 'Hakuro-nishiki'.

early 1990s it was in practically every nursery in the Pacific Northwest. It immediately
became a must-have shrub but disappeared
from the scene just as quickly. It is probably overhyped, but we find it very attractive

most of the year. In early spring we prune
our plants hard down to 1 foot (0.3 m). The
stems grow very quickly to 4–5 feet (1.2–1.5
m) by late summer and in fall turn a nice
reddish color; they aren't as showy as those

of some of the other red-stemmed willows but are pretty nonetheless. The leaves emerge in early spring almost totally pink, are pink and white with a little green later in spring, and are mostly green with some white and pink in summer. The pink and white highlights are present from spring until fall. To increase these colors, selectively prune the plant in midsummer. Hardy in zones 5–8. Grow in sun.

Salix lanata. We first saw this excellent willow at Beth Chatto's glorious garden in Norfolk, England. It took a long time to find a plant, but it was worth the effort. It can grow to 4–5 feet (1.2–1.5 m) tall over many years but is slow to get to 2 feet (0.6 m). Ours is a multistemmed, bushy, small shrub. The gray-green leaves are the main reason to grow this fine shrub; they are oval and can be as wide as they are long. The internodes on the stem are short, so the plant is fully covered with the leaves. So far we haven't had any catkins on our plant, but we assume they will be similar to those of other shrubby willows. Our plant grows in very damp conditions, but we have also seen plants growing along with rhododendrons that need good drainage. Hardy in zones 3–8. Grow in sun to partial shade.

Salix nakamurana var. ***yezoalpina.*** This low-growing native of Japan is excellent for cas-

Salix lanata.

cading over a wall or growing in a sunny garden. One of our plants thrives in very sandy soil in blazing all-day sun. *Salix nakamurana* var. *yezoalpina* gets up to 1 foot (0.3 m) tall and grows to perhaps 6 feet (1.8 m) wide. The stems flow over the soil, following the contours of any rocks. The leaves are fairly large and oval, with deeply impressed veins that create a leathery look, and in spring are covered with woolly hairs. The foliage remains deep green all summer and turns yellow in fall before dropping. The catkins are 2 inches (5 cm) long and upright. This variety blooms after the leaves expand in spring, making a pretty combination of fuzzy gray leaves and yellow catkins. Overall it is an easy-growing, adaptable ground cover that will add textural interest to the garden. Hardy in zones 4–8. Grow in sun to partial shade.

Sambucus (elderberry)

Members of this genus can make beautiful foliage plants or fruiting plants. We have grown elderberries in our garden for years for their serrated leaf margins and various leaf colors, from golden yellow to white-spotted, purple, or green. The leaves are compound and pinnate. The flowers are white or pink in early summer and can be attractive if there is room to grow a large plant. We prune our plants very hard in winter to ensure large leaves and full, bushy growth. This involves

Salix nakamurana var. *yezoalpina*.

sacrificing the flowers, but we believe the better foliage more than makes up for it. We have seen some unpruned elderberries in gardens that were the size of a small tree, up to 20 feet (6 m) tall.

Origin: Europe.
Hardiness: Zones 5–8.
Exposure: Sun to partial shade.

Sambucus nigra Black Beauty ('Gerda'). This fairly new plant from England has very large, glossy, deep purple leaves that are almost black in spring. It is incredibly fast growing: the first plant we saw, in Northeast Portland, grew from a 1-gallon container plant to an upright 10-foot (3 m) shrub within three years, with huge leaves 12–16 inches (30–41 cm) long. The flowers are pink in early summer and up to 10 inches (25 cm) across. This easy, fast grower is an excellent background plant for the perennial border. We have grown *Clematis viticella* through our plant; its blue flowers show up nicely against the deep purple foliage. Hardy in zones 5–8. Grow in sun.

Sambucus nigra Black Lace ('Eva'). Like *S. nigra* Black Beauty, this selection has deep purple foliage, but whereas Black Beauty has broad leaflets, Black Lace has finely cut leaflets. Black Lace also has a smaller, more arching habit than the more upright growing Black Beauty. The flowers are rich pink in early summer and would nicely echo some of the early summer–flowering perennials. With selective pruning, Black Lace will make an excellent specimen plant in the garden or in a container. Hardy in zones 5–8. Grow in sun.

Sambucus nigra 'Pulverulenta'. White-splashed foliage is the major reason to grow this fun plant, which is much different from *S. nigra* Black Beauty and *S. nigra* Black

Opposite: *Sambucus nigra* Black Beauty.

Sambucus nigra Black Lace.

Lace. We aren't usually fans of splashed variegation, but 'Pulverulenta' is so distinctive—startling, almost—that we feel it is well worth growing. Each spring we cut back our plant to about 4 feet (1.2 m). The new growth is especially spotted with white. We suggest combining this cultivar with *Clematis texensis* hybrids for a pretty splash of bright pink in summer. Hardy in zones 5–8. Grow in sun.

Sarcococca (sweet box)

These Asian shrubs are evergreen, and all bloom from winter into early spring. They can be 1–4 feet (0.3–1.2 m) tall; most are suckering shrubs that grow much wider than tall. The foliage is narrow, lance-shaped, and glossy deep green year-round. The flowers are small puffs of stamens appearing in late winter; they remain unnoticed except for their wonderful sweet fragrance, which carries well and can be detected over 100 feet (30 m) away on a mild day. The flowers are followed by shiny black fruit in fall.

Origin: Asia.
Hardiness: Zones 6–9.
Exposure: Partial shade.

Sarcococca hookeriana var. *digyna* 'Purple Stem'. A looser, more open grower with purple stems and petioles. Our plants have been much slower growing than the species. Hardy in zones 6–9. Grow in shade.

Sarcococca hookeriana var. *humilis*. This Himalayan native is the lowest-growing sarcococca we've seen. Our three plants have been in the ground for twenty years and are 1 foot (0.3 m) tall and 10–12 feet (3–3.6 m) wide. The green leaves are glossy year-round and make a good backdrop for the sweetly scented flowers and fruit. This easy-growing ground cover is a good choice for the shaded garden. We grow our plants under magnolias, and they make perfect companions. Hardy in zones 6–9. Grow in shade.

Spiraea

These plants come from a wide range of locations throughout the Northern Hemisphere and are easy to grow in many climates as long as they are given adequate moisture. For us, the *S. japonica* hybrids, which are the most common in gardens, are difficult. They also look bad after flowering, as they hold onto their flower clusters. Many of the newer hybrids have glowing yellow, gold, or orange foliage with pink flowers that are just too garish. We have selected two cultivars that offer beautiful foliage and flowers.

Origin: Northern Hemisphere.
Hardiness: Zones 3–10.
Exposure: Sun.

Spiraea betulifolia 'Tor'. This small-growing ornamental from Asia can get to 2 feet (0.6 m) tall. Its small, serrated, oval leaves are deep green all summer. The high point is in fall when the leaves turn brilliant yellow, orange, and red for a long period. Small clusters of white flowers appear in midspring all over the plant. This excellent little shrub grows best in full sun and doesn't get big enough to need to be pruned, unlike many other spiraeas. Hardy in zones 3–9. Grow in sun.

Spiraea thunbergii 'Ogon'. This golden-leaved spiraea from China offers lacy foliage for the garden. It gets to 4–5 feet (1.2–1.5 m) tall but can be selectively pruned to 3 feet (0.9 m). The stems are thin and flexible and move with the breeze. The leaves, which are 2 inches (5 cm) long and ¼ inch (0.6 cm) wide, are lush golden yellow from spring through summer, turning bright yellow in fall. Very small white flowers are borne along the stems in early spring like the old-fashioned bridal wreath spiraea (*Spiraea prunifolia*). Hardy in zones 3–9. Grow in partial sun.

Stachyurus 'Magpie'

Our first plant of 'Magpie' came from England and turned out to be the understock. Then in 1980 when Roger went to England, he saw plants of it but not in any nurseries. After many tries we finally received scion wood and had it grafted. This cultivar looks just like *S. praecox* but has lovely medium green leaves with a broad creamy white margin touched with pink. It seems to be more tender for us than the species, but we saw a glorious plant in the Asian Collections at the U.S. National Arboretum.

    Origin: China.
    Hardiness: Zones 7–8.
    Exposure: Partial shade.

Stachyurus praecox

This strangely beautiful deciduous shrub always receives comments from visitors to our garden. We have seen plants in the Portland area that are 15–19 feet (4.6–5.8 m) tall and at least as wide. The growth is a very strong, upright vase shape. The leaves are 4–6 inches (10–15 cm) long, serrated, and medium green all spring and summer, turning yellow and pink in fall for a pretty end to the season. The flowers are long, stiff spikes that hang down. The yellow individual flowers are small, but the spikes can be up to 10 inches (25 cm) long. It's fun to use *S. praecox* in cut-flower arrangements, as the cuttings can be placed to show the spikes growing horizontally. *Stachyurus praecox* occasionally dies back in our garden after a freeze, so we grow it

Stachyurus 'Magpie'.

Stachyurus praecox.

against a hedge or building for a little more protection. It can be a very striking specimen.

Origin: Japan.
Hardiness: Zones 7–8.
Exposure: Partial shade.

Vaccinium glaucoalbum

This wide-spreading evergreen shrub grows to about 18 inches (45 cm) tall and 36 inches (91 cm) wide. The irregular growth needs some light pruning to create a fuller plant. For a good part of summer the oval, deeply veined leaves are bluish green with a white indumentum underneath; from fall through winter they are burgundy and purple. Early spring brings racemes of pinkish white flowers that are attractive but not overly showy.

These are followed in fall by small black fruits. *Vaccinium glaucoalbum* is an excellent foliage plant for the woodland garden. We grow ours in filtered shade along with rhododendrons and other shrubs.

Origin: China.
Hardiness: Zones 6–9.
Exposure: Partial shade.

Vaccinium 'Sunshine Blue'

This blueberry hybrid is among our favorite plants, both for its ornamental appeal and for its delicious fruit. We first heard about it from J. C. Raulston back in the 1980s. Reaching 4–5 feet (1.2–1.5 m) tall over many years, it forms a multistemmed shrub with fine branches that give it a light texture. Its deciduous foliage is narrow as with most blue-berries, but with a bluish tint that lasts all summer. In late fall the leaves turn rich red-purple, and they hold on for a good portion of winter (zone 7). In warmer climates the foliage might be almost evergreen. Soft pink, urn-shaped flowers appear in midspring.

By midsummer, later than most blueber-ries, 'Sunshine Blue' begins to bear a good amount of sweet fruit. If you want a large crop all at once, this cultivar isn't for you. But it is a good choice if you simply want enough blue-berries for a salad or on your morning cereal. We have had other blueberries in the garden, and the birds strip them of fruit as soon as the berries ripen. Not so with 'Sunshine Blue'. Since this selection fruits for a month or more, there are only a few ripe berries at any one time, so the birds seem to leave it alone.

In short this shrub has almost everything a gardener could want: superb flowers, foli-age, and fruit. It grows in full sun or semi-shade and does fine in either Los Angeles or Michigan.

Origin: Garden origin in the eastern
    United States.
Hardiness: Zones 5–10.
Exposure: Sun to partial shade.

Viburnum

Like *Rhododendron*, this genus is of great or-namental value and offers a large range of plant types, from 20-foot (6 m) shrubs to 18-inch (45 cm) dwarf forms, including de-ciduous and evergreen foliage types. Various plants flower at various times year-round. For instance, our plants of *V. plicatum* f. *tomento-sum* 'Summer Snowflake' are still blooming in midfall just before *V.* ×*bodnantense* 'Dawn' begins its winter bloom.

Viburnums may have clusters of small flowers like those of *Viburnum farreri*, medi-um flowers like the *V. carlesii* group, larger ster-ile flowers like *V. opulus*, or lacecap flowers like *V. plicatum* f. *tomentosum* 'Summer Snow-flake'. The flowers can be greenish at the be-ginning of their bloom, then white or pink depending on the species or hybrid. Not all viburnums fruit, but those that do can be very beautiful. The fruit appears in fall in colors ranging from yellow to red, blue, and black.

All viburnums seem to be adaptable and easy to grow. In our area, many grow with very little summer water. It's amazing to see plants of *Viburnum davidii* survive in the hor-rendous places people put them. Just think how wonderful this plant could be with some care and attention.

Origin: Europe, Asia, eastern United
    States.
Hardiness: Zones 5–9.
Exposure: Sun to partial shade.

***Viburnum* ×*bodnantense* 'Charles Lamont'.** We have grown this excellent hybrid for twenty-five years and become more im-pressed each winter. It is several steps showier than *V.* ×*bodnantense* 'Dawn'. Where 'Dawn' blooms sporadically from fall until spring, 'Charles Lamont' holds on until midwinter to open its showy pink flowers. The flowers are also darker pink than those of 'Dawn' and appear in much greater profusion for at least a month. Our plant is an upright 8-foot (2.4 m) shrub with dark green leaves. For a smaller garden, 'Charles Lamont' makes a

The showy pink flowers of *Viburnum ×bodnantense* 'Charles Lamont'.

handsome, fragrant addition. Hardy in zones 5–9. Grow in sun to partial shade.

Viburnum ×bodnantense 'Dawn'. This selection eventually becomes an open 15-foot (4.6 m) shrub. The foliage isn't showy, but the leaves are deeply veined dark green from spring through fall. Flowers begin showing color in midfall and continue until early spring. The flower clusters are about 2 inches (5 cm) across, light pink to white, and distinctly fragrant. The individual flowers can be frozen, but the overall effect through winter is wonderfully cheerful. Hardy in zones 5–9. Grow in sun to partial shade.

Viburnum ×burkwoodii 'Mohawk'. This hybrid was introduced by Don Egolf at the U.S.

National Arboretum. Its rich pink buds are followed by lovely early-spring flowers that are light pink to white (despite a photograph of 'Mohawk' frequently seen in catalogs that was taken using a pink filter, making it look as though the open flowers are dark pink). The flowers are deeply cinnamon-scented. This upright shrub grows to 10 feet (3 m) tall. The foliage is deep green and slightly glossy. Hardy in zones 4–8. Grow in sun.

Viburnum carlesii 'Compactum'. This bushy deciduous shrub is less than half the size of the species, getting to 6 feet (1.8 m) tall and 4 feet (1.2 m) wide over many years. The leaves are dark green and oval with light hairs on the upper sides. The flower's buds are light pink and fade to white in early spring.

Viburnum dilatatum 'Michael Dodge'.

The two-toned buds and flowers are attractive and form a cluster 3 inches (7.5 cm) across. The cinnamon scent of the flowers is powerful on warm spring days. In summer the dark green foliage makes an excellent foil for *Clematis florida* var. *sieboldiana* (syn. *C. florida* 'Bicolor') or other small summer-flowering clematis. Hardy in zones 4–8. Grow in sun.

Viburnum dilatatum (linden viburnum). This Japanese native is ornamental at least two seasons per year. The white flowers show up in late spring and are followed by red or yellow fruit in fall. *Viburnum dilatatum* can grow to 6–12 feet (1.8–3.6 m) tall and forms a many-branched shrub. The oval leaves are deep green from summer until fall. On our plants, the fall color is yellow with red to purple highlights. The flowers are borne in clusters 3–4 inches (7.5–10 cm) across. Most of the *V. dilatatum* cultivars have red fruit, but *V. dilatatum* 'Michael Dodge' has golden yellow fruit. Hardy in zones 5–8.

Viburnum dilatatum Cardinal Candy ('Henneke'). A typical *V. dilatatum* in size and plant form. The red fruit is incredibly showy when it covers this 8-foot (2.4 m) shrub in fall. Said to fruit well even without a pollinator. This cultivar survived –30°F (–34°C) when all the other *V. dilatatum* seedlings perished. Hardy in zones 4–8. Grow in sun.

Viburnum dilatatum 'Michael Dodge'. We first saw this selection, named for plantsman Michael Dodge, at Stonecrop Gardens in Cold

Spring, New York, and were immediately taken by its heavy crops of lovely golden fruit that appear in early fall. It took several years to find plants for our own garden. We have been told that *V. dilatatum* 'Michael Dodge' will fruit better with another *V. dilatatum* planted nearby for cross-pollination. Hardy in zones 4–8. Grow in sun.

Viburnum 'Molly Schroeder'. This cultivar is said to hold the pink flower color longer and better in the southern United States than *V. plicatum* f. *tomentosum* 'Pink Beauty'. Hardy in zones 4–8. Grow in sun to partial shade.

Viburnum plicatum 'Pink Sensation'. We have grown this excellent plant since the 1980s

Viburnum plicatum 'Pink Sensation'.

and consider it one of the most beautiful viburnums. Our plant came from our friend Connie Hanson, to whom we remain greatly indebted. (Connie is no longer with us, but her garden in Lincoln City, Oregon, is now open to the public.) Jack Richards of Salem kept asking if we had 'Pink Sensation' and eventually sent cuttings from Connie's plant. After rooting several plants, we saw how wonderful this selection is and planted a specimen of our own, which is now 10 feet (3 m) tall and 8 feet (2.4 m) wide. It grows in full sun most of the day but has an open growth habit that forms a perfect framework for the purple-green spring leaves. When the blooms appear they look like pink popcorn balls covering the tops of the stems and foliage. The flowers are soft pink and in our garden hold their color for two to three weeks. 'Pink Sensation' is easy to grow in full sun to semishade and is hardy in zones 4–8.

Viburnum plicatum f. tomentosum 'Pink Beauty'. We regularly see lacecap viburnums in gardens throughout the United States, but they usually have white flowers. 'Pink Beauty' is a lacecap with light pink flowers. This native of China and Japan has several upright trunks that grow to 10–12 feet (3–3.6 m) tall, with side branches growing horizontally to 6–8 feet (1.8–2.4 m) across. The deeply veined foliage is purple as it emerges and turns deep green in summer. The flowers are 2–3 inches (5–7.5 cm) across and appear above the leaves in late spring, holding their color for at least three weeks; they are composed of lots of fertile florets and several sterile larger flowers. Our plants of 'Pink Beauty' are real showstoppers in spring and make a good background for colorful perennials during the rest of summer. Hardy in zones 4–8. Grow in sun to partial shade.

Viburnum plicatum f. tomentosum 'Summer Snowflake'. We strongly recommend this Japanese native as it is easy to grow, hardy (zones 4–10), and showy in bloom for seven to eight months a year. Although we were originally told it would only reach 6 feet (1.8 m) tall, our plants are 12 feet (3.6 m) tall and 5–6 feet (1.5–1.8 m) wide. They are multi-trunked, with horizontal side branches, and are consistently more upright than spreading. The foliage is typical of *V. plicatum* f. *tomentosum* cultivars, but the dark green leaves are about half the size. The flowers appear in midspring, clothing the plant in a shawl of white, and continue blooming sporadically until the first hard frost.

'Summer Snowflake' seems to laugh at sun and heat. We grow it in full sun in Oregon, and we have seen plants in full sun in central California where temperatures reach 100°F (38°C) through much of summer. When grown in the shade, this selection grows to be much wider than tall.

Another cultivar from Japan, *Viburnum plicatum* f. *tomentosum* 'Nanum Semperflorens' (syn. 'Watanabe'), is said to be very different. However, although it is supposedly a smaller grower, we have seen it in a range of sizes, and the flowers are identical to those of 'Summer Snowflake'. We wonder whether 'Nanum Semperflorens' just came from cuttings taken of slower-growing wood than 'Summer Snowflake'.

Opposite: Blanketed in white flowers, *Viburnum plicatum* f. *tomentosum* 'Summer Snowflake' makes a stunning backdrop for various

Viburnum 'Pragense'. This very hardy, fast-growing evergreen comes from Prague and was named in the 1950s. It is a cross between *V. rhytidophyllum* and *V. utile*. An upright grower to 10–12 feet (3–3.6 m) tall and 6 feet (1.8 m) wide, it makes an excellent screen or individual plant throughout much of the United States. 'Pragense' can grow extremely fast and should be pruned to make it bushier. The leaves are glossy, dark green, and deeply veined, with a light-colored indumentum underneath. White flowers appear in small clusters in late spring. So far we haven't seen any fruit on our plants. We can't understand why we don't see this pretty foliage plant in more gardens. We planted several 1-foot (0.3 m) plants for our brother in heavy clay among large tree roots; they not only survived but thrived. Hardy in zones 4–9. Grow in sun to partial shade.

Weigela

Old-fashioned *W. florida* has gone through a makeover by breeders and offers some great foliage and flowering plants for the modern garden, ranging in size from large shrubs 6–8 feet (1.8–2.4 m) tall to plants just 2 feet (0.6 m) high. The multitrunked branches of weigelas form irregular, open shrubs. The dwarf forms are much more full growing and can be pruned to fill in even more. The foliage is usually 2–3 inches (5–7.5 cm) long and 1/2 inch (1.25 cm) wide, depending on the variety. Foliage color can differ dramatically from selection to selection, ranging from purple, yellow, and green to variegated yellow or pink, among other combinations. Flowers vary as well; they can be subtle white, pink, or purple, or dramatic rich red, purple, or yellow. The combination of flowers and foliage can be quite shocking or very subdued. It seems the sky is the limit for weigela breeders.

Weigelas are being bred with beautiful foliage and flowers, but many are just green through summer. To remedy the late-spring bloom, try planting an annual vine into whatever weigela you grow.

Origin: Japan, Korea, northern China.
Hardiness: Zones 4–8.
Exposure: Sun.

Weigela 'Candida'. A 6- to 8-foot (1.8 m to 2.4 m) shrub with medium green foliage. The flowers are snow white with a lemon yellow throat in mid to late spring. Grow in sun.

Weigela florida Wine and Roses ('Alexandra'). A low grower to 3 or 4 feet (0.9 or 1.2 m) tall with foliage that is deep purple from spring through summer and small flowers that are rich pink in midspring. Grow in sun.

Weigela 'Looymansii Aurea'. This cultivar has bright yellow foliage all summer without the harsher tones of *W.* 'Rubidor'. Soft, light pink flowers complement the foliage. Grow in sun.

Weigela 'Red Prince'. This American hybrid has deep green leaves that make a great foil for the deep rich red flowers in spring.

Opposite top: *Zenobia pulverulenta*, center, distinguishes itself in the garden with its dusty blue foliage.

Opposite bottom: It is debatable whether *Zenobia pulverulenta* 'Blue Sky' has better blue foliage than the species.

Too bad it doesn't bloom at Christmastime, as the foliage and flowers would be perfect for the holiday season. Grow in sun.

Weigela 'Rubidor'. Many people think the golden yellow foliage with orangish highlights is wonderful with the red-purple flowers. The combination can be garish or glorious, depending on your perspective. Grow in sun.

Zenobia pulverulenta (dusty zenobia)
This blueberry relative and *Vaccinium* 'Sunshine Blue' provide our last foliage color each fall. Its leaves, which appear late in spring, are oval and about 1–1½ inches (2.5–4 cm) long; they are a beautiful dusty blue all summer and turn an excellent yellow-red in late fall. *Zenobia pulverulenta* grows to 3–6 feet (0.9–1.8 m) tall depending on the amount of sun or shade it receives. We site our plants in partial to full sun, and they grow into multistemmed bushy shrubs. The flowers are white bells appearing on 4- to 6-inch (10 cm to 15 cm) stalks in late spring; they are very showy for two to three weeks and lovely against the blue foliage. This excellent, moderate-growing, deciduous shrub is beautiful from midspring until early winter, when it finally loses its leaves.

In addition to the species, we grow 'Blue Sky'. It is said to have better blue foliage, but to us it looks like the species we acquired from Bovees Nursery in Portland, Oregon, in the 1980s. Bovees must have had a particularly good form. Both the species and its cultivars are excellent shrubs.

Origin: Eastern United States.
Hardiness: Zones 5–9.
Exposure: Partial shade.

Hardiness Zones

Temperatures

$$°C = 5/9 \times (°F{-}32)$$
$$°F = (9/5 \times °C) + 32$$

USDA Plant Hardiness Zones
Average Annual Minimum Temperature

ZONE	TEMPERATURE (DEG. F)			TEMPERATURE (DEG. C)		
1	Below −50			−45.6 and below		
2a	−45	to	−50	−42.8	to	−45.5
2b	−40	to	−45	−40.0	to	−42.7
3a	−35	to	−40	−37.3	to	−40.0
3b	−30	to	−35	−34.5	to	−37.2
4a	−25	to	−30	−31.7	to	−34.4
4b	−20	to	−25	−28.9	to	−31.6
5a	−15	to	−20	−26.2	to	−28.8
5b	−10	to	−15	−23.4	to	−26.1
6a	−5	to	−10	−20.6	to	−23.3
6b	0	to	−5	−17.8	to	−20.5
7a	5	to	0	−15.0	to	−17.
7b	10	to	5	−12.3	to	−15.0
8a	15	to	10	−9.5	to	−12.2
8b	20	to	15	−6.7	to	−9.4
9a	25	to	20	−3.9	to	−6.6
9b	30	to	25	−1.2	to	−3.8
10a	35	to	30	1.6	to	−1.1
10b	40	to	35	4.4	to	1.7
11	40 and above			4.5 and above		

To see the USDA Hardiness Zone Map, go to the U.S. National Arboretum site at http://www.usna.usda.gov/Hardzone/ushzmap.html.

Shrubs for Specific Sites and Purposes

Small shrubs for sun—to 3 feet (0.9 m) tall

Berberis calliantha
Berberis thunbergii 'Bagatelle'
Berberis thunbergii 'Concorde'
Berberis thunbergii 'Gold Nugget'
Chaenomeles ×superba 'Cameo'
Chaenomeles ×superba 'Hollandia'
Clethra alnifolia 'Hummingbird'
Comptonia peregrina
Fothergilla gardenii 'Jane Platt'
Ilex crenata 'Dwarf Pagoda'
Itea virginica 'Henry's Garnet'
Mahonia nervosa
Rhododendron kiusianum
Salix lanata
Spiraea betulifolia 'Tor'

Shrubs with exceptional foliage

Acer palmatum 'Shishigashira'
Acer palmatum 'Ukigumo'
Aralia elata 'Aureovariegata'
Aralia elata 'Variegata'
Azara microphylla 'Variegata'
Choisya ternata 'Aztec Pearl'
Choisya ternata 'Sundance'
Comptonia peregrina
Cornus alternifolia 'Argentea'
Cornus sericea 'Hedgrows Gold'

Cotinus coggygria Golden Spirit
Cotinus 'Grace'
Disanthus cercidifolius
Fatsia japonica
Fothergilla ×intermedia 'Blue Shadow'
Hydrangea aspera subsp. *sargentiana*
Itea ilicifolia
Lonicera nitida 'Baggesen's Gold'
Loropetalum chinense 'Sizzling Pink'
Mahonia ×media cultivars
Osmanthus heterophyllus 'Goshiki'
Osmanthus heterophyllus 'Sasaba'
Physocarpus opulifolius Coppertina
Pieris 'Bert Chandler'
Rhododendron 'Golfer'
Rhododendron proteoides
Salix integra 'Hakuro-nishiki'
Sambucus nigra Black Lace
Spiraea betulifolia 'Tor'
Stachyurus 'Magpie'
Zenobia pulverulenta

Shrubs for deep shade

Aucuba japonica 'Rozannie'
Buxus sempervirens 'Variegata'
Eleutherococcus sieboldianus 'Variegatus'
Fatsia japonica
Hydrangea anomala subsp. *petiolaris*
  'Platt's Dwarf'
Mahonia bealei

Mahonia ×*media* 'Charity'
Mahonia nervosa
Sarcococca hookeriana var. *digyna* 'Purple
  Stem'
Sarcococca hookeriana var. *humilis*

Shrubs for full sun

Berberis calliantha
Berberis thunbergii f. *atropurpurea*
  'Helmond Pillar'
Berberis thunbergii 'Bagatelle'
Berberis thunbergii 'Concorde'
Carpenteria californica 'Elizabeth'
Comptonia peregrina
Cytisus battandieri
Fothergilla gardenii 'Jane Platt'
Fremontodendron 'California Glory'
Ilex crenata 'Dwarf Pagoda'
Ilex crenata 'Sky Pencil'
Lavatera ×*clementii* 'Barnsley'
Lavatera thuringiaca 'Ice Cool'
Lespedeza thunbergii 'Gibraltar'
Loropetalum chinense 'Sizzling Pink'
Magnolia stellata
Poncirus trifoliata
Rhamnus frangula 'Asplenifolia'
Rosa glauca
Rosa rugosa
Salix nakamurana var. *yezoalpina*
Spiraea betulifolia 'Tor'

Fragrant shrubs

Abeliophyllum distichum
Chimonanthus praecox
Chionanthus virginicus
Choisya ternata cultivars
Clethra alnifolia
Clethra barbinervis
Comptonia peregrina
Corylopsis cultivars
Cytisus battandieri
Daphne species and cultivars
Hamamelis species and hybrids
Heptacodium miconioides
Illicium anisatum (foliage)
Illicium floridanum (foliage)
Lonicera fragrantissima
Magnolia Kosar/de Vos hybrids
Magnolia liliiflora
Magnolia sieboldii
Mahonia bealei
Mahonia ×*media*
Osmanthus species and hybrids
Philadelphus
Poncirus trifoliata
Ribes sanguineum (foliage)
Rosa rugosa
Sarcococca hookeriana
Viburnum ×*burkwoodii* 'Mohawk'
Viburnum carlesii 'Compactum'

Index